What Thought Leaders Are Saying About The Intentional Accountant:

"Accounting isn't just a task or a skill set, or even a job. It can be a calling, and a mission and a lifestyle. In the utterly useful *The Intentional Accountant*, Darren Root provides the playbook for transforming what accountants can and should become. Highly recommended!"

—Jay Baer, *New York Times* best-selling author of *Youtility*

"Darren is a true visionary and has successfully translated his expertise within *The Intentional Accountant*. The book offers a step-by-step guide for positively transforming every area of firm operations—from attracting the right clients and deploying cutting-edge technology to building a brand, assembling the right staff, and creating a rich culture."

—Jon Baron, Managing Director, Professional Segment, Tax & Accounting, Thomson Reuters

"A firm's ability to quickly adapt to new technologies and more efficient practice management methods can mean the difference between transforming their firm into a thriving business or being left behind. *The Intentional Accountant* offers practitioners a clear roadmap to guide them."

—Brad Smith, president and CEO, Intuit Inc.

"Success is rooted in true intention. Darren's ability to distill the key elements that help firms transition into thriving, profitable businesses is proven and well-known. This new book serves up these elements and guides you through the steps required to build your Next Generation Accounting Firm with focused intention—a formula that has worked for hundreds of firms across the country."

—René Lacerte, CEO and founder of Bill.com

The
Intentional
Accountant

Your Roadmap for Building a
Next Generation Accounting Firm®

published by

Other titles by M. Darren Root:

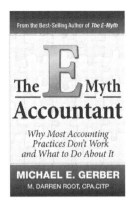

Youtility for Accountants: Why Smart Accountants Are Helping, Not Selling, by *New York Times* best-selling author Jay Baer and Darren Root

The E-Myth Accountant: Why Most Accounting Practices Don't Work and What to Do About It, by Michael E. Gerber and Darren Root

Published by RootWorks, LLC.

1516 South Walnut Street, Bloomington, IN 47401 USA

ISBN 978-0-692-20700-0

This book is dedicated to my mom.

For each of us life presents a series of challenges, some good and others not so good. My mom, through her daily actions, taught me to approach each new day with a positive attitude no matter the circumstances. I never fully understood what a great gift this was until she was no longer here for me to thank in person.

Thanks, Mom!

My hope for all of you is that you will look at each new day with your glass half full.

Joanne J. Root, 1931-2008

Acknowledgements

Over the course of my career, one of the most important lessons that I've learned is the value of a great team. It's because of my outstanding staff, at both RootWorks and Root & Associates, that I've been able to live the life that I desire—working as a true entrepreneur and enjoying life outside of work with friends and family.

I would like to first thank my business partners, Wade Schultz and Ryan Deckard for the countless hours they've spent with me in strategy sessions and working with committed focus to build a successful brand for both businesses, but for more importantly being my dearest friends.

I would also like to offer a special thank you to my friend and other business partner, Kristy Short Ed.D—without her, this book (and past books) would not have been possible.

And finally, a heartfelt thanks to my family and my faith for unconditional support and guidance at every step of the long and arduous road of life. I thank my three grown children, Andy, Meredith, and Alex; watching you grow up was a wonderful blessing, and now sharing life with you as adults is a true gift. And lastly to my wife of more than 30 years, Michelle, whom I've had the pleasure of knowing since we were kids. Your love and friendship is a constant reminder of the best part of my life and the reason my glass remains full.

The Intentional Accountant

Your Roadmap to Becoming a
Next Generation Accounting Firm®

Table of Contents

When I began my career in the accounting profession more than 30 years ago, I never dreamed that I would one day be writing a book, much less a third one.

As an accountant, my role had nothing to do with writing, and much less to do with questioning the traditions of my chosen profession. My job, as it was defined for me, was to do the work that paid the bills, just as my father had done in his firm. There came a point during those early years, however, when I realized that running a firm in the traditional mode and adhering to the staid accounting "brand" just wasn't for me. Working long hours tethered to my desk never felt right; it went against my entire being. And I know, from talking with hundreds of my fellow accounting professionals over the years, that I am not alone in this feeling.

Through my tenure as Executive Editor of *CPA Practice Advisor* magazine, CEO of RootWorks, and co-author of *The E-Myth Accountant* and *Youtility for Accountants*, I've had the privilege to speak with hundreds of accountants across the United States—many of whom I am now proud to call my friends. The people I have come across in our profession are among the kindest and most well-intentioned of any I have ever met. And, just like I did so many years ago, many of them struggle to find the balance between having an accounting firm and having a life.

That's why I wrote this book. I want to share my experiences and offer the principles and practical steps that I took to build what I call a Next Generation Accounting Firm. My intention is to make the journey easier for my colleagues. My intention is to help you.

Before we get started on how to build a Next Generation Accounting Firm, let's take a moment to offer some background on where the term came from and define what it really means.

Several years ago, while I was out presenting to the profession at a variety of education-based events, I recognized that there was a major disconnect between where the profession was—and where, as accounting firm owners, we needed to be. Where we needed to *be* was actually in direct opposition with long-standing traditional methods of operating an accounting firm. It was then that I realized we needed a way to clearly explain to the profession what an accounting firm could be—what I call a Next Generation Accounting Firm.

I believe that there are two aspects of the Next Generation Accounting Firm: the technical and the emotional.

The technical level is composed of several pieces and parts—those elements that make the business "run." I'm referring to technology, workflow processes, staff, clients, marketing, branding, and everything in between. These are the elements that I will detail throughout this book as I share tips on creating a blueprint for your own Next Generation Accounting Firm.

On an emotional level, this term means something very different, defined by the passion and pride that I feel for my business today. It is a term that symbolizes the sum of all the individual pieces and parts come to fruition.

With all this in mind, I believe a Next Generation Accounting Firm is:

> A business built on focused intention with unmitigated entrepreneurial spirit that enables you to have the life you want. It runs on a business model that supports an environment where you can be *present* in all aspects of your personal and professional lives to have the greatest impact on family, staff, clients, and community. A business that operates independent of you; creates a better working culture for your firm; offers security through recurring revenue; fosters creative thinking; evokes excitement with each new stage of evolution; inspires the next generation of professionals; and is built for transition to support your legacy.

The concept of building a Next Generation Accounting Firm is the foundation on which RootWorks was established: an organization dedicated to helping other accounting firm owners realize their dream of entrepreneurship.

Ultimately, this book is about getting your life back by staying focused on your Next Generation Accounting Firm journey.

As members of the accounting profession, we are all connected. Personally, I am passionate not only about the ability that we, as accountants, have to help our clients, but also about how we can help each other. My hope is that this book will inspire you to look at your firm differently—to see your business as a moldable piece of clay that you can design and massage into something beautiful and inspiring. A masterpiece that not only supports the life you desire to live, but serves to inspire and enhance the lives of your clients. I hope that you will be motivated to make the changes required to renew your passion in order to truly *lead* your business and, ultimately, find the freedom to enjoy your life and the people in it.

I firmly believe in the power of living with intention—taking the reins and creating the life you want...making things happen...not simply adhering to a model that you've been told is the right one. Today, however, too many accountants are still unintentional about their business, allowing their firms to run on autopilot as they keep their heads down in day-to-day technical work. I know from personal experience that this is no way to operate your firm...it's no way to live. My goal for you, by the time you finish reading this book, is to realize the awesome opportunity you have to create something truly special: a business you will be proud to call your own.

The good news is that you've taken your first step toward becoming intentional about how you operate your business. By simply selecting this book, you have created the intention to transition to the role of a true entrepreneur by building your Next Generation Accounting Firm. Your journey begins today, and I'm excited to make it with you.

Sincerely,

M. Darren Root, CPA, CITP, CGMA

As a CPA and self-proclaimed "software geek," I have been following Darren Root and his contributions to the accounting profession for many years. When I first heard him speak about how technology would change the lives of practitioners, I knew that he was on to something—something big—a revolution that would transcend the status quo solutions that had served firms so well…up until now. Today, with the publication of this book, I can see that my forecast was spot-on.

Little did I know that only a few years after meeting Darren at an educational event, I would be calling him a close colleague—and, even more unexpectedly, writing the foreword to his third book. I am honored to do so. Darren is someone who brings an enormous amount of positive energy and insight to my firm and my life—energy that was very much needed to help me transition my business into a Next Generation Accounting Firm.

In 2013, I worked 3,400 hours in my firm. Patty, my "first mate," worked 2,400 hours. My brother John worked 2,600 hours.

I used to think that this was just the price that we had to pay in order to provide the appropriate level of service to our clients. But—and this was a huge epiphany for me—Darren changed my mindset about how I was managing my firm and my life.

For years, I have been working as a technician *in* my firm, doing whatever it takes to keep the workflow going and juggling numerous duties with the hope of keeping all the balls in the air. I was working an exhausting schedule just to maintain operations, and all without a proper vision or a business model in place. All this added up to an exceptionally poor work-life balance. Through Darren's guidance, and as an example of a practitioner that was successful in his Next Generation Accounting Firm journey, I now understand, I mean really understand, that in order to have the business and the life that I want, I need to be intentional about it.

Shortly after meeting Darren, I joined his organization, RootWorks, as an Academy member. That's when I really took grasp of his vision for member firms like mine. The scope of this vision is so much bigger than simply staying up-to-date on the latest practice management solutions. It is to help our profession transition away from outdated traditions and, subsequently, enable practitioners to transform from technicians to entrepreneurs with focused intent and purpose.

Darren has helped guide me to the realization that in order to have the firm and the life that I want, I need to embrace the processes and people (clients included) that add positive energy to my firm's culture—and avoid those that subtract from it.

Through Darren's counsel and my membership in RootWorks, I have found the encouragement and practical tools I need to not only change my practice, but also to change my life. This may seem unbelievable to some of you who have not yet made the shift to this way of working and living, but it is true.

What Darren has offered me is what I hope to offer my own clients: the information and insights that will make a profoundly positive impact on their businesses and their lives. I have heartily embraced the fact that we only live once and that we need to focus on having a rich experience in the world and sharing that with those who are significant to us.

It is one thing to acknowledge that family and work-life balance should be of primary concern in life. However, so often in public accounting, these ideals can become lost in waves of paper and client work. With RootWorks, and now with *The Intentional Accountant*, Darren offers us concrete best practices to achieve the transition to operating a Next Generation Accounting Firm, transforming ourselves from technicians to entrepreneurs in the process.

I have been in the accounting profession for close to four decades. I understand, as Darren does, how intimidating adopting new technology and new business models can be—especially to an established firm. However, thanks to Darren, I also understand how essential it is to embrace new ways of doing business, because our clients are also expecting us to change. This has all led to even greater questions for me, both of which Darren addresses thoroughly and eloquently in the book:

> How do we cross the great divide between the old way and the new way?

> How do we manage both the stress and the promise of change?

Darren has the management expertise and experience to demonstrate how to cross over safely and with confidence by clearly defining what's important and what isn't. Within this book, he shares how to transition from a traditional technician role to that of a true entrepreneur. From my own experience, I have learned that Darren's approach is both practical and effective—allowing me and my staff to follow a progressive path with clear benchmarks and proven processes for "doing it right."

Darren offers sage advice in the first chapter of this book:

> *"Logic tells us that there is no reason to hold on to the ways of the past. If you are a business owner, whether you are in the accounting profession or not, your health, your relationships, and the prosperity of your business cannot be sustained if the way you run your business is completely out of sync with the vision you have for your life."*

I decided to follow Darren's advice and implement a new business model for my firm. Part of this process involves using my marketing prowess to find clients that match my ideal profile and letting go of some clients whose needs do not match the unique skill sets within my firm. I am also divesting myself of a portion of my practice to reduce my working hours so that I have time to think, relax, plan, and prepare for what is next. If I hadn't met Darren, I am quite certain that I would have continued to work the same insane schedule, cheating myself out of the personal and professional life I want and deserve.

Of course, as with any significant change, there is much work to be done. As I transform my practice to a Next Generation Accounting Firm and continue to become more intentional in my role as an entrepreneur, I know I can meet the challenge of change. I know that with the roadmap Darren has laid out in this book, I will be able to make my vision a reality.

I am so grateful for Darren's willingness to share his insights and experience with our profession. I have no doubt that if you take the time to read and engage with the exercises in *The Intentional Accountant,* your firm and your life will be better for it.

Best regards,

Tom

Thomas P. Abrassart, CPA, CFP
President, Longwood CPA
Longwood, FL

CHAPTER 1

The Moment of Truth: Are You Intentional or Unintentional About Your Business?

"Your time is limited, so don't waste it living someone else's life. Don't be trapped by dogma – which is living with the results of other people's thinking. Don't let the noise of others' opinions drown out your own inner voice. And most important, have the courage to follow your heart and intuition."

– Steve Jobs

In his classic book, *Innovation and Entrepreneurship*, business guru Peter Drucker wrote, "The entrepreneur always searches for change, responds to it, and exploits it as an opportunity."

I'll be honest; when I launched my firm almost 30 years ago, I don't know that I would have understood what this meant. I know now that if I had read Drucker's book prior to starting my business, I would have been much better prepared to lead as an entrepreneur. I also would have understood how to take advantage of change, turning it into new opportunities for growth, rather than let it overwhelm and control me.

Like many of you, I launched my firm without any real entrepreneurial training. They didn't teach this stuff when I was in business school. If they had, it may have saved me many years of feeling unfulfilled, exhausted, and frustrated by the demanding, time-draining life of a small business owner where my business just happened to me; where I operated without intention.

I know now what Drucker meant: true entrepreneurs are in constant pursuit of progress and are always striving to get better at what they do. Entrepreneurs take change in stride, learn from it, and then recalibrate the business model to exploit the opportunities that come from positive change. Of course, this is nearly impossible to do if you are always wrapped up in the details of getting work done and are unable to stand back and evaluate how your business needs to evolve.

Like so many business owners, I built my business around my core skill set (i.e. I am a CPA, so I'll do tax returns, create financial statements, etc.). I started out by putting myself in the role of technician, relegated to frontline work for several years. It never occurred to me that I should be intentional about every aspect of my business. I accepted the mindset that being overworked and having to "do it all" was the price I had to pay for being a small business owner. In reality, I was as far away from being an entrepreneur as you could get. I found myself feeling more and more unfulfilled and began to question my "do-it-all-alone" mindset. My only hope arose from considering that there must be a better way of doing business.

If you can relate to that feeling of being overwhelmed, as John Abrassart expressed in the foreword of this book—but feel like you can't do anything about it because your business model centers solely around what you do—my hope is that this book will inspire you to make the transition from practitioner to entrepreneur. That is, someone who stops dreading and avoiding change, and instead "always searches for change, responds to it, and exploits it as an opportunity." Running your business as a true entrepreneur opens the door to true work-life balance and enables you to love both your business and your life.

Thinking back, the seed of my "do-it-all-alone" mindset was planted during my childhood in Bedford, Indiana, as I watched my father work endlessly in his own accounting firm. It took me until my mid-thirties to see that I could change my situation. Once this belief took root in my conscious mind, I felt empowered to begin my journey toward creating a business that supports the life that I want to live, rather than trying to work my life around the demands of being a business owner—running an unintentional firm.

My journey would eventually lead me to not only become a successful entrepreneur with my accounting firm, but also to establish Root-Works, a company dedicated to helping other accounting firm owners adopt the Next Generation Accounting Firm business model and realize their dream of intentional entrepreneurship. Today, hundreds of accounting firms across the United States are applying the Root-Works model to significantly improve their productivity and profitability. This book applies the core principles of this model to offer you a personal roadmap to becoming a true entrepreneur while freeing yourself from business practices that are no longer working for you. While this book addresses Intentional Entrepreneurship from the perspective of accounting professionals, the concepts within transcend industry boundaries.

I reached my breaking point during a bleak winter in 1997. Looking back, I can easily recall how my firm was sucking the life right out of me. It was the dead of winter in the middle of tax season when I reached my limit—that breaking point when I had to make a choice. I could keep doing what I was doing and work all hours of the day and night, or I could find a new way of doing business. I am happy to report that I did the latter, discovering the joy and satisfaction of being an entrepreneur and thoroughly enjoying my life.

The day of my epiphany is burned into my brain—the day I realized that there had to be a better way to run my business. I woke up at 3 a.m., having tossed and turned most of the night, thinking of all of the work I had to do. At that point, sleep seemed futile, so I got up and headed to the office, leaving my wife and three kids sleeping soundly. As I made the 30-minute drive to the office, I found myself actually looking forward to several hours of early-morning quiet time. No, I didn't like spending more time at work than I did at home, but I needed a chance to plow through the tax returns that had been piling up.

As a CPA, most of my days during the busy tax season were spent in appointments with clients. That meant I had to complete client work during the quiet hours—early in the morning and late at night. That January morning started with me being jolted awake at 3 a.m. I worked until after 6 p.m., and then headed back home to pick up my family to attend my oldest son's basketball game over an hour away. It was almost 11:30 that night when I finally made it home—exhausted. I headed to bed knowing that I would do pretty much the same thing all over again the next day.

This would be my life for years: working what seemed like endless hours during tax season. Then once things settled down in late April, it would take me another couple of months to recalibrate my life and achieve a sustainable schedule…only for the mania to start all over again the following January.

Some people thrive on a crazy work schedule—running constantly just to keep up with the demands of their business and not having time for the things that life is really about. For me, the most important aspects of my life—family and faith—were being neglected. I wasn't *thriving* at all. At best, I was *surviving* on a day-to-day basis. My life was passing me by quickly and I had to make a change.

As I mentioned earlier, I had grown up in a traditional accounting firm—literally—watching my dad put in all the long hours. Being enslaved to the firm was all I knew, because I had watched my father run his practice exactly the same way. My father routinely got up at 4:30 each morning, made the same 30-minute drive to the office, worked all day, and then raced home to attend family events. He spent Saturdays at the office, and after church on Sunday, he sat at a card table in our family room…you guessed it—working.

Long, hard hours were the norm for my dad. His mindset: if there is work to be done, you get it done. This is how I, too, saw the accountant's world. Yet despite the foreshadowing of my own future as a firm owner, I chose to enter the profession.

I started by earning my degree from Indiana University. Perhaps it was a little bit of my future entrepreneurial spirit shining through, because even in college, I wanted my financial independence. I worked 30 hours a week at a high-end men's clothing store near campus called Whitesides. While the job helped me pay for school, it also provided a great training ground. I learned how to strike up a conversation with a complete stranger, finding some commonality that would put the potential customer at ease and allow me to make the sale. I learned the importance of dressing well to create a positive personal brand, and learned how critically important the client experience is to customer perception. I also met many of Bloomington, Indiana's professional leaders, several of whom would become clients of my future firm, Root & Associates.

After I graduated, I did what all of my fellow accounting graduates did and took a job with a then Big 8 accounting firm, Deloitte Haskins and Sells. I interviewed with a couple of small firms, which I was drawn to, but the idea of working for one of the largest firms in the world had greater appeal to a young, recently married guy who hadn't spent much time outside of southern Indiana. Still, during my time at Deloitte, I continued to feel an overwhelming desire to control my destiny, to be creative, and to build my own business.

With entrepreneurship calling me, in 1987, my wife, pregnant with our first child, and I moved back to Bloomington. Within a few years, I had formed Root & Associates and was on my own.

As a CPA, opening an accounting firm seemed like the obvious path. In the first few years of running my firm, though, any illusion that I had of being in control of my schedule and my life quickly faded. I soon realized that I was not only following in my father's footsteps as the owner of my own accounting firm, but I was also bearing every bit of the weight that he had carried. I worked long hours, accepting any client who came through the door, did most of the work myself, and failed to develop a standard system for all staff to follow. I had created an unintentional business. To say that I felt trapped was an understatement—I felt completely overwhelmed and I saw no way out of the "life" I had created.

I was, quite frankly, frustrated by the fact that my dream had turned into a technician's nightmare. I knew there had to be a better way to do things, but I had no idea how to incite change. In the traditional accounting profession, you aren't rewarded for innovation; you are rewarded for production. More output equals more income—even if increasing your output means seriously diminishing your quality of life. The issue for me was that, in my heart, I knew that the traditional route wasn't the most efficient or productive way to run a business. I knew it was time for a change, but had no idea where to start.

Because I was unsure of my first step, I did my research, turning to a few business sages for advice. I started by studying Stephen Covey's *The Seven Habits of Highly Effective People*, even becoming a facilitator and training others in Covey's strategies. At the highest level, *7 Habits* helped me realize that it was within my power to choose the type of firm and life I wanted. It was *my* choice. Just acknowledging that I could change things was incredibly freeing and empowering.

Beyond this broad epiphany, I honed in on a single and crucial Covey concept: the necessity for creating a clear vision for the life I wanted to live. This concept, coupled with the understanding that it was my decision to make, gave me the footing I needed to start my journey toward entrepreneurship and build my desired life. I want to be clear that this concept is critical to your journey as well. I highly recommend that if you haven't already, you read Covey's *The Seven Habits of Highly Effective People* as part of your transformation.

Core Covey Concept: Have a clear vision for your best life

Before I defined the vision for my business—and, ultimately, for the life I wanted to lead—I was essentially running a firm by making up the rules as I went along. I was not intentional. Without a vision of where you want to go, you can easily end up meandering along instead of living and working with meaning.

Covey instructs people to "begin with the end in mind." Before jumping in feet-first, you have to be able to envision your life and your business. To really define your vision, you have to create it mentally, put it in writing, and then work to build the business that supports your vision. Taking the time to develop my vision was a huge part of my success in transforming my firm and my life.

About the same time I was learning from Covey, I was also studying Michael Gerber's *The E-Myth*. Gerber's book triggered another "a-ha moment," enlightening me to the fact that there is a world of difference between being an entrepreneur and being a technician. It was clear to me that I had spent most of my working life as a technician—a frontline producer of tax returns, financial statements, and any other work that our clients requested. This is what had been modeled by my dad's business, and this is what I saw when I looked around at many accounting firms. I knew that while being a technician is a noble pursuit, it wouldn't lead me to the place I aspired to be—an entrepreneur running a successful business and living a balanced, quality life.

My life as a technician left me exceptionally frustrated. While I was "in charge" I had absolutely no freedom. I was tied to the office, head down, producing. It was when I started to mold my vision and write it down that I felt the transition begin. My vision made me realize that I needed to work with intention on my business in every aspect, as opposed to just cranking out work all day long. Even bigger than this was the realization that I had to lose the guilt. I had spent so many years equating "work" with producing an actual product that when I stopped spending all of my time completing product, I felt as if I weren't really "working." I had to learn to let that go, something I discuss in greater detail in Chapter 12.

Creating a vision, losing the guilt…it all led to one thing—a change in mindset.

My new way of thinking allowed me to redefine my role from technician to entrepreneur. This meant spending time strategizing for growth, building the right team, standardizing processes, defining my ideal clients, building a great brand, integrating web and mobile technologies, and becoming intentional about every aspect of my vision. This also meant knocking off at a decent hour to go home and recharge my batteries. As an entrepreneur, I learned to trust my instincts, which meant putting an end to the doubt and fear—defeating that voice that now and again tried to convince me that my new way of doing business was wrong and that I would fail.

As I grew in my new entrepreneurial role, there were days when I would drive home during busy season at 6 p.m. and notice the lights on at all the other accounting firms. I would go home to my family, attend my kids' games, and relax. I felt a considerable amount of guilt and insecurity at first, telling myself that I should really be producing more work. The reality was that I *was* working. I had simply figured out a way to work more efficiently and cut down the crazy hours, so there was no reason to feel insecure.

Logic tells us that there is no reason to hold on to the ways of the past. If you are a business owner, whether you are in the accounting profession or not, your health, your relationships, and the prosperity of your business cannot be sustained if the way you run your business is completely out of sync with the vision you have for your life.

We live in an amazing time in history. Technology has leveled the playing field between large organizations with many resources and smaller ones with far fewer. There are so many tools that allow us to work faster and smarter. Having the time to research and lead implementation of the right technologies to support your new business model is another reason to let go of the technician role that may keep you trapped and stagnant.

Before you take your first step on the road to becoming an intentional entrepreneur, I want you to keep some key questions in mind:

- Are you operating the kind of business you really want? Is your business designed around the type of life you want to lead, or is your life designed around your business?

- Have you taken the time to "begin with the end in mind?" Have you clearly articulated all the goals you have for the key areas of your life?

- Are you operating your business from a technical or an entrepreneurial perspective? In other words, do you spend most of your time working *in* your business or working *on* your business?

- Have you embraced technology in a way that helps you achieve your goals, or has it just made your life more complicated?

- Are you approaching every aspect of your business with intention, or are many aspects of your firm unintentional?

- Have you identified the Sweet Spot for your business—the right mix of clients, systems, and people? And do you manage your firm to stay balanced within this "sweet" zone? So important is this concept to your Next Generation Accounting Firm journey that I've dedicated a detailed section to it below.

Moving Along the Next Generation Continuum

As we move through this book, there is another element I want you to consider thoughtfully. I want you to think of being an intentional entrepreneur as working on a continuum, not as an all-or-nothing process. Few of us will ever be purely entrepreneurs or purely technicians. The goal is to move further down the spectrum from working exclusively in your business, to working on your business most of the time.

You will know when you've evolved into an intentional accountant and are managing an intentional firm when you experience a culture that enables you to relax and be present in all aspects of your firm. It is this type of environment that, in turn, allows you to be present in all aspects of your life and have the biggest impact on family, friends, staff, and clients. This is the very essence of your Sweet Spot.

Finding and Staying in Your Sweet Spot

As I said, your journey is a continuum. And on that continuum your goal is to move away from being a technician and toward being an entrepreneur. As I also said, you will never be purely a technician or purely an entrepreneur—the trick is to find the right balance between the two...that place on the continuum where you are able to live the life you desire—this is your Sweet Spot.

By operating a Next Generation Accounting Firm, I've found my Sweet Spot—that place where I can be ever present in my firm without the business relying on me to be there every minute of every day.

Implementing advanced technologies, building the right staff, serving my ideal clients, and building a powerful brand are all elements that enabled me to reach Next Generation status and achieve the right balance between technician and entrepreneurial work. And this is where I plan to stay.

Everyone will have a different "equation"...and different place on the continuum that serves as their Sweet Spot. To put it in numbers (we are accountants after all), I would say that for me it's 75 percent entrepreneurial work and 25 percent technician. This is where I fall on the continuum. For others it may be 60-40 or 80-20. Whatever the equation, the key is to be closer to the entrepreneur end of the continuum. Only there will you enjoy the immense value of living within your Sweet Spot.

A word of caution: once you achieve the right balance and find your Sweet Spot, there is no resting on your laurels. You have to continue to protect it. There are many things that will work to throw you off balance—the wrong staff and clients, outdated solutions, an inability to delegate...and the list goes on. Your job is to stay the Next Generation course, work as an entrepreneur on your firm, and remain true to your vision. Trust me, once you've reached your Sweet Spot, you'll know it, and you will do whatever it takes to stay there.

Now, it's your turn. Let's get started by thinking about the vision you have for your business—and more importantly, your life.

CHAPTER 2

It All Starts With You – Getting Clarity About What You Want

"It is the people who figure out how to work simply in the present, rather than the people who mastered the complexities of the past, who get to say what happens in the future."

– Clay Shirky

As I mentioned in the last chapter, Stephen Covey's *The 7 Habits of Highly Effective People* had a profound effect on my life. Habit 2, "Begin with the End in Mind" is one of my favorites. The key concepts here that ring true for me are that:

> "I can choose my own future and create my own vision of it," and

> "I will create results mentally before beginning any activity."

In my experience, "beginning with the end in mind" is an exceptionally challenging exercise for most people. When I make presentations across the country about building a Next Generation Accounting Firm, I often ask attendees if they have a written vision for their firm. Although I know, from my own experience, that this is one of the most important exercises in building a successful business, typically, only about 15 percent of respondents have completed this task. Creating a vision allows you to stop and think through what it is you really want, and with this exercise comes great clarity on the results you want to achieve. From here, you are in a better position to build the right staff, implement the right technologies, standardize the right processes, and educate your clients on the best way to work with your firm. That's right; you are in the driver's seat for how your clients work with your firm.

Essentially, the most effective people are those who shape their own future and don't allow others or circumstances to determine their destiny. Effective leaders mentally plan and then physically create positive results. It's the vision that you create in your head and write down on paper that shapes your future. This vision sets the stage for your end goals, and is the first step to becoming intentional about your business.

The concept of "begin with the end in mind" applies to many different areas of life. In this chapter, we are going to focus on work. Ask yourself what it is you really want out of your work. This process is not easy, it takes time, and it takes dedicated, deep thought.

I have spent a great deal of my career working on my firm, Root & Associates, a CPA firm that I founded nearly 30 years ago. Today, I am still the managing partner of Root & Associates, which is most certainly not the same firm it was decades ago. In the following chapters, I will use my firm to provide real-world examples of how the concepts in this book can be applied to transition a legacy firm into a thriving next generation business.

As I mentioned in Chapter 1, when I started Root & Associates, I knew I had a defined skill set: the technical knowledge of a CPA. Based on this, I went about growing my client base as quickly as I could, offering services based on my skills and taking on any client who walked through the door. The critical point here is that I had no end in mind. I only knew that I wanted to grow my business and survive. I was unintentional from the very beginning. Sound familiar?

This situation usually occurs out of necessity, but the approach is problematic when it becomes your business model. This model—which is really no model at all—leads firm owners down the path of creating a business that is completely dependent on them. Sooner or later, the business owner feels trapped, overwhelmed, and frustrated, with retirement as the only foreseeable escape. But why would you ever want to build a business that enslaves you, where your only out is growing old enough to be free of it? The ultimate goal, of course, is to develop a business that can run smoothly no matter the level of your involvement. This not only frees you to work strategically on your firm, but over time, also sets you up for a smooth, positive transition into retirement—on your terms.

As a CPA and trusted advisor, I have worked with hundreds of small business owners over the past 30 years, including electricians, doctors, attorneys, restaurateurs, and other CPA friends—most of whom share this issue. When you build a business around you and your skills, you create a path with no defined point for change. You grow; you work harder. You grow some more; you work harder. It's a vicious cycle.

For me, the turning point came when I had been running Root & Associates for about 10 years. I had a lot of clients who depended on me to do their work. Yes, I did have staff, but ultimately the clients depended on me personally because that is how I set up my business. At the time, I also had three children who were highly active in extracurricular activities, and I was deeply involved in my community. Pile on trying to keep up with a rapidly changing profession and all the things required to stay current—complex software solutions, staff training, marketing and branding—and I was drained. I kept asking myself, "Where do I find time for my personal life?"

I felt out of control, because I failed to start with the end in mind. I was on the fast track, of sorts, but I had no idea where it was leading. It was a track I needed to alter.

As I prepared to write this book, I revisited the work I did back in 1997, the year I began transitioning my thinking and my life. For a week, I sat on a beach in Longboat Key, Florida, thinking and soul searching. I started by writing down what I wanted to accomplish with my business and for my life. The following are the notes from that week on the beach, which have become the foundation for how I now live my life:

- To live my life aware that who I am is as much what others see as it is what I believe.

- To live my life without excessive indulgences—aware that my mind, my body, and my family are my only true assets.

- To deal with others with honesty, integrity, tolerance, and compassion.

- To dedicate my remaining years to helping others find purpose in their lives, insuring that my influence on others is consistent with my values and principles.

- To live my life with purpose and apply all of my potential.

- To build a business that supports my life and not a life that supports my business; leading my organization to be self-perpetuating, with a rich learning environment, and not dependent on me as the primary technician.

This is my list. Now, I encourage you to invest the time in writing your own. Try to think about what you want out of your life. Don't limit yourself by thinking about the barriers that may stop you from achieving what you want. I have found that if you give yourself time and space to genuinely tap into your innermost desires and dreams, few of them are unreachable. Allow yourself to think big, and dig deep to find the vision that will guide you to not only being a better business owner, but also a more fulfilled human being.

It was clear to me that although I had built a profitable business over that 10-year span, it didn't align with the vision I had for my life. As Albert Schweitzer once said, "Success is not the key to happiness; happiness is the key to success. If you love what you are doing you will be successful." My business required me to be the main focus, the person who everything revolved around. I was a technician by day and a business owner by night. It was a simple truth: there was not enough of me to go around. Two key questions loomed in my mind:

1. How was I supposed to go from where I was to where I wanted to be?

2. How could I take my existing business and transform it into the opportunity I desired?

The answer: systematically and methodically, with determination and intention.

To begin, it's important to understand the core challenges in my business. From there, we'll move into a phased approach to addressing these issues.

Core Challenges

Within my firm, Root & Associates, I identified many issues:

- Our client base was diverse and spanned many different industries, which meant we could never be great at serving any one industry or truly develop our core competencies.

- We supported several services—some that were outside of our core competencies, some that we were moderately good at fulfilling, and others that were squarely in our wheelhouse.

- We took every client who walked through the door because I had yet to define my firm's vision and identify who my ideal clients were. I did this to keep revenue flowing in, not because we had our end in mind.

- I created a business model where many clients were solely dependent on me being involved, at some level, to complete their work.

- We lacked standard processes and procedures—meaning that every client was served differently and the client drove our processes. It also meant that staff lacked clear direction on the best way to perform their jobs.

- Our brand was unintentional—there was nothing that clearly differentiated us from other accounting firms.

After going through the "begin with the end in mind" exercise, I mapped out the vision for my firm:

- Create a business operated by a team, not just me, and within a collaborative environment.

- Offer services based on our core competencies—the services at which we excelled.

- Build a business composed of our ideal clients.

- Apply effective marketing and branding to attract qualified leads to keep the sales funnel full and insure focused growth.

- Serve select industries in which we had extensive expertise.

- Operate within a business model/defined system to deliver services efficiently, instead of the client driving our processes and the services we offered.

- Build a brand that I would be proud to represent.

- Use technologies that enables our team to work any time and from anywhere.

The Opportunity

As you can see, the wide chasm between where Root & Associates was and where I wanted it to be, meant that we needed a plan to begin to re-engineer the business. The following is a three-step, high-level strategy that I developed as a first step to start redefining my business. I encourage you to take out a pen and complete this three-part exercise before moving on.

1. **Make a list of services, clients, and industries.** Take a complete inventory of your firm. Write down all of the specific services your business performs, the type of cli-

ents you serve, and the industries you support. *(See Step 1: Core Competencies on the accompanying worksheet.)*

2. **Evaluate your list.** Review your newly created business inventory and ask yourself which of the services and client industries you feel confident serving. Identify those that support your core competencies. For example, if you currently perform audit services, but don't feel audits are a core competency, remove auditing from your list. If you have only a couple of construction clients and don't feel comfortable with your firm's knowledge in that industry, remove that industry. *(See Step 2: Areas of Goodness on the accompanying worksheet.)*

3. **Define who you want to serve.** This is a critical step in your evolution. Evaluate your list from step 2 with the goal to reach clarity on the types of clients you most want to work with. Ask yourself: 1) What are the industries that I really enjoy serving, and are these industries that I can serve as an expert? 2) What are the services I want to provide these industries, and are these services that fall within my firm's core competencies? When you are done, you should have a clear list of qualified clients who you want to serve and who you can serve exceptionally well. If these clients comprised your database, you would truly have your ideal clientele. *(See Step 3: Areas of Greatness on the accompanying worksheet.)*

After completing this exercise, what you have in front of you is the beginning of your vision statement. From this point, you should be ready to discuss the next component of your vision: your business model.

As we leave this fundamental chapter, remember that great leaders don't stay the course when the status quo is not working. Pausing to create and articulate your vision before moving on will prepare you to transition from a technician in your firm to working on your business as a focused, effective, and intentional entrepreneur.

Firm Vision | Step 1: Core Competencies

Make a list of all of the services your firm currently offers. Be thorough.
(Examples: 1040s, audits, 990s, payroll, etc.)

1. _____	11. _____
2. _____	12. _____
3. _____	13. _____
4. _____	14. _____
5. _____	15. _____
6. _____	16. _____
7. _____	17. _____
8. _____	18. _____
9. _____	19. _____
10. _____	20. _____

Make a list of all of the industries your firm currently serves. Again, be thorough.
(Examples: physicians, non-profits, construction, etc.)

1. _____	11. _____
2. _____	12. _____
3. _____	13. _____
4. _____	14. _____
5. _____	15. _____
6. _____	16. _____
7. _____	17. _____
8. _____	18. _____
9. _____	19. _____
10. _____	20. _____

Firm Vision | Step 2: Areas of Goodness

Of the services on the previous page, list those that you consider your firm to be 'pretty good' at providing:

1. _____
2. _____
3. _____
4. _____
5. _____
6. _____
7. _____
8. _____
9. _____
10. _____

11. _____
12. _____
13. _____
14. _____
15. _____
16. _____
17. _____
18. _____
19. _____
20. _____

Of the industries you serve, list those for which your firm has a good level of knowledge:

1. _____
2. _____
3. _____
4. _____
5. _____
6. _____
7. _____
8. _____
9. _____
10. _____

11. _____
12. _____
13. _____
14. _____
15. _____
16. _____
17. _____
18. _____
19. _____
20. _____

Firm Vision I Step 3: Areas of Greatness

From your list of services in Step 2, which services is your firm great at providing—which represent your distinctive core competencies?

1. _____
2. _____
3. _____
4. _____
5. _____
6. _____
7. _____
8. _____
9. _____
10. _____

From your list of industries in Step 2, which ones are those for which your firm provides great service—which represent your distinctive niche industries?

1. _____
2. _____
3. _____
4. _____
5. _____
6. _____
7. _____
8. _____
9. _____
10. _____

CHAPTER 3

Getting it *Right*: Building Your Next Generation Business Model

"Whatever the mind of man can conceive and believe, it can achieve. Thoughts are things! And powerful things that, when mixed with definiteness of purpose, and burning desire, can be translated into riches."

– Napoleon Hill

The accounting profession has become technologically complex over the years. Many of today's practitioners aren't sure how to make decisions on technology solutions, the most efficient way to connect internal systems, or which best practices to implement. The thing to remember here is that you need to adopt the solutions that best fit your current and future needs. You may have used one solution in a different firm that isn't right for your current business. Don't be concerned with cutting costs. Focus instead on analyzing which solutions are best for your particular business.

Based on your work in Chapter 2, you are now ready to proceed with the next phase of creating your vision statement. It's time to build the right business model—one that is intentional; one that will free you to spend more time working as an entrepreneur in your business. Let me be clear: an effective business model is a core element that should be tightly integrated within the framework of your vision. Think of your business model as the blueprint from which you and your team will work to accomplish the goals you have set within your vision.

Be patient and remember that the building and implementation of your business model is a phased approach that will not happen overnight. No matter how motivated you are to enact changes immediately, it's probably not possible to fix all of your issues in the short-term. Improving all areas of operation—including defining services, building a delivery system, training staff, and even training yourself to change your way of thinking—will take time to do correctly. The idea is to create your blueprint, then consistently progress toward building a business model that evolves around your staff delivering services more effectively. Your plan should also enable you to create more and more "space" in your life. Over time, you will continue to create even more room for yourself to work on your business. Take a deep breath and proceed at a comfortable pace, celebrating the small successes along the way.

As you start down this path, it's important to realize that—like it or not, intentional or accidental—you already have a business model. For example, your clients may drive your current business model. This occurs when you allow clients to decide how you deliver services to them. This is what I call a "business model by default" or the "unintentional business model." And unfortunately, it's how many firms operate today.

Years ago, I operated under a default business model—quite unintentionally.From the start, I failed to lead my clients in the direction I knew they should go. Instead, I allowed clients to define my firm's processes—so they were leading me. My unintentional business model came about, primarily, because we took on any client who walked through the door—no matter what service was needed or no matter what industry they were in. This limited me and my staff from becoming experts in any one market or service area. Additionally, delivering services based on each client's unique needs meant that service delivery had to be customized for every client. This barred me from establishing standardized firm wide processes and obligated my staff to understand every client's custom workflow. Clearly, this model presented numerous challenges for Root & Associates. It also kept me working, endlessly, in my firm because I was usually the guy with all the answers.

The absence of uniform processes for handling client work put significant pressure on me personally. Each time we took on a new client, I had to be intimately involved in order to understand exactly how service would be delivered. And because our services were so wide-ranging, rather than being tailored to the type of clients and industries we wanted to work with, once again, I was the go-to guy.

The problem is, if all aspects of your business rely on you, then you will continue to have the same issues that small business owner Tom Abrassart described at the beginning of this book. Like me and Tom, you will continue to be a main producer of work without time for impacting your business at a higher strategic level.

If your firm is like the vast majority of accounting firms—90+ percent have 10 or fewer employees, including their ownership—you likely already understand how an efficient business model supports higher productivity and profitability.

Let's pause a moment to look at the six elements of a defined business model, as based on my experience:

- A defined list of service offerings.

- A defined list of the types of clients your business will serve.

- A trained, qualified staff that clearly understands the business model and their individual role in it.

- A clearly defined delivery system for each of the services offered.

- Standardized processes and procedures for every aspect of your business that clearly articulate uniform workflows.

- A highly efficient technology infrastructure that supports your business model.

You may have already realized that we have discussed the first two items in this list in the last chapter.

The third item, developing a trained and qualified staff, is something that we will address in Chapter 6. The remainder of this chapter focuses on the remaining three elements: 1) building a delivery system, 2) creating standardize processes and procedures, and 3) building a technology infrastructure.

With these building blocks in place, you position yourself for long-term success and sustainability. Over the next few pages, I'm going to delve into these three elements in more detail.

1. Build a clearly defined delivery system.

Having a defined delivery system for each service offered is key to achieving freedom and transitioning into the role of entrepreneur. Without this, practitioners are at the mercy of clients to define their own unique delivery system. This will negatively affect firm efficiency, profitability, and the quality of service delivery. Having a defined service delivery system in place will also provide your staff with the structure they need to perform their work competently.

Consider Starbucks as an example of how a standardized delivery system offers immense value. Picture what happens when you walk into Starbucks to place an order for a latte:

- You walk up to the cash register, place your order with the cashier, and pay for it.

- The cashier writes your order instructions and name on the side of your cup and then passes the cup to the barista.

- The barista fills your order using the company-standard recipe and process.

- Your name is called and you collect your latte.

It's a simple, uniform process that ensures that millions of latte drinkers get the right order, in a timely fashion, every time. While there is nothing overly complicated or special about this process, it does illustrate three important points: 1) Starbucks provides you with a menu of choices; you are not in charge of what they offer; 2) each person in the system knows what to do to get your order ready—without Starbucks' CEO Howard Schultz working the counter; and 3) as the customer, you don't have to do a thing to guide the process. The end result is an inherent trust that Starbucks' experts will fulfill your order properly.

My intent here is not to offer a direct process comparison between ordering a latte and providing accounting services. Clearly, a firm's processes are far more complex. My point in offering this example is to emphasize the ease and efficiency a standardized process delivers for both the business and its clients.

Now, with the Starbucks example in mind, ask yourself: Is this how service delivery looks in my business? If your answer is "No," you're in good company: most accounting firms haven't taken the time to perfect their end-to-end service delivery. Often, so much of your time is spent working in your firm that you're left with little to no spare time to make intentional changes, even those that would enhance operations. I like to say, "you've been too busy driving to stop and get gas."

Payroll services offer a great example of the pitfalls that come with an "unintentional business model." Consider the following example:

- The firm has no consistent process for setting up a new payroll client.

- The firm has no consistent method for adding new employees into the payroll system; client information is delivered in whichever manner they choose to submit it (email, fax, letter, or phone call).

- There is no efficient and consistent way of gathering employee hours to process payrolls. The hours are delivered in inconsistent, various ways.

- The firm prints payroll checks for some clients and uses direct deposit for others.

- Clients' employees receive paper check stubs and/or electronic stubs in emails or portals, depending on what they prefer.

- When it comes to sending payroll reports to clients, the methods are equally varied. Some are sent digitally to a portal, some take the form of printed reports, and others are emailed.

The point is, most accounting firms allow their clients to define the process.

Imagine if Starbucks ran the same way. Say that, instead of moving through the expected ordering process at Starbucks, you brought your own coffee and coffeemaker and then instructed the barista on how to make your latte using your tools. It sounds ridiculous, but believe me: the hundreds of firm owners I talk to each year indicate that they do not have a defined delivery system in place. They want to lead clients effectively, but are inadvertently allowing the clients to lead the process.

Consider another example of the damage caused by allowing clients to control your processes. Has your firm ever agreed to work around a new or existing client who uses an old version of QuickBooks®? Take a minute to review just a few of the issues this can cause:

- An accounting firm works with clients on multiple desktop versions of QuickBooks. Instead of using the collaborative cloud-based model with real-time data entry and the ability to work with clients in an anytime-anywhere environment.

- The client has promised a backup of data each period, but often doesn't send it on time—meaning the client controls when work can begin.

- You are forced to clean up the "digital garbage" you receive, which often results in a great deal of lost time and energy.

- With each new period, the firm discovers changes to historical information, after cleaning up the file from the prior period.

Added up, it's an equation for a lot of time wasted—which isn't a desirable business model for firm or client.

If your clients are creating inefficiencies in your practice, frustrating your staff, and keeping you tethered to a process that isn't working, you owe it to yourself, your family, and your employees to stop trying to adapt to the situation. Instead, use your energy to build the business model that will offer you flexibility and freedom.

I can tell you first-hand that building a standardized delivery system is hard work. It takes time and demands that accounting professionals stay apprised of leading solutions, trends, and best practices. It's not realistic to expect that you can continue spending all of your time working in your firm and still have time to implement the changes needed to build your ideal business. I understand this very common problem.

Some days, you may not even feel like you have time for lunch, but trust me: getting outside of the four walls of your office and finding ways to collaborate with other like-minded entrepreneurs can be a huge help in this regard. The process of working with other motivated practitioners who are also destined to be intentional entrepreneurs is incredibly valuable. My recommendation is that, in addition to following the steps laid out in this book, you also seek out peer-to-peer networks to support your efforts.

2. Create standardized processes and procedures.

Another key component of your business model is the standardization of your firm's processes and procedures.

Just like Starbucks has a process for ensuring that customers receive a custom latte each time, an accounting firm needs to have clearly defined processes for every routine operation. When this occurs, the staff works in concert, performing work in the same, uniform manner—no matter which staff member is handling the work, and no matter which client is being served.

Think about the process of taking on a new client. What does that process look like for your firm today? Is it standardized? Does your staff complete project tasks the same way every time, so that the outcome is predictably consistent? Do you have a form (digital or printed) that you complete each time to set up a new client? Do you have a standard process for taking that form and creating the client in your system?

At Root & Associates, we use a standardized form for new client set-up, performed by a defined staff member. Our process is simple:

- The client is added to our practice management system, which seamlessly integrates with Microsoft Outlook so that all of the information is immediately available on our mobile devices as well (smartphones and tablets).

- The client is added to our online document management system, providing them with online access through our client portals.

- The client is then added to other relevant "spaces" based on the services they need such as tax, bookkeeping, and payroll.

- All client data points are seamlessly integrated.

Standardization of routine processes and written procedures are essential to building consistency and autonomy for your staff. The time that you invest in designing your business model, training staff, and implementing the plan will pay great dividends. With a defined delivery system in place, you can create consistency and delegate with confidence.

Consider every aspect of your firm and create a standardized process. The following are a few examples of areas to standardized to help get you started:

- New client setup.

- Online access for clients.

- Standard naming conventions for all aspects of your practice, including document management and client demographic information.

- Standard forms to support administrative processes (e.g., tax routing sheet, new client setup form, payroll setup form).

These are just a few examples. There are most certainly many more to be identified and developed.

3. Build a highly efficient technology infrastructure.

A discussion about developing an ideal business model needs to include technology. As I mentioned in Chapter 1, there has never been a better time, from a technology standpoint, to be in the accounting profession. We have the opportunity and freedom to work anytime, anywhere, and from any device. We are no longer tethered to our desks.

As technology evolves, so must the way accounting firms deliver services by meeting the needs of clients and staff. With so many solutions available, it's important to evaluate each potential solution in terms of: 1) how it will help support your business model, 2) how it will support your clients (client-facing solutions), and 3) how it will support your staff (back-office solutions).

I know building a technology ecosystem may seem overwhelming. After all, your skill set may not even currently include technology. The reality is that in today's Next Generation Accounting Firm, technology is crucial. However, it doesn't have to be overwhelming if you can master a few key concepts and organize your thinking.

The first key concept is collaboration. I believe that this is one of the most important concepts to grasp as you consider the technologies that will comprise your technology infrastructure. Collaboration encompasses working with others to achieve shared goals. This is at the heart of how you should be serving your clients, as well as how you should be working with your staff. As such, collaboration should always be front-of-mind when evaluating solutions for your ecosystem.

When considering a technology solution, ask yourself: Does this solution support collaboration? Think of collaboration as having access to information and solutions at any time, from anywhere, and on any device. What better way to operate than with full access to all data and to all individuals (clients and staff) within your system?

The following are three examples to help illustrate this point:

1. Let's go back to our QuickBooks example. Assume that your client uses the QuickBooks desktop application and that data files reside on the client's PC. Considering the concept of collaboration, should this solution be part of your ecosystem? The answer is "No." Why? Because the criteria of any time, anywhere, and from any device cannot be met if data resides on your client's computer. However, the answer is not to throw out QuickBooks as the solution; it is the top solution among small businesses, after all. The answer is to find an alternative to meet the requirements of collaboration. This can be accomplished using an authorized QuickBooks hosting provider or implementing QuickBooks Online. What I want you to take from this example is that clients are required to work in the collaborative accounting solution(s) that you choose for them. This must be part of your business model.

2. Now let's assume that you've transitioned your client to hosted QuickBooks to meet the collaboration requirement. Your staff now has real-time access to client data, but to complete the project the staff member is working on requires a copy of a document for an asset purchase. This document is a hard copy in the client's file cabinet. Does this support your collaborative strategy? Again, the

answer is "No." The next step would be to digitally attach client files to QuickBooks transactions for immediate access at anytime. This requires an online document management system that integrates with QuickBooks, so staff can access attached documents from either application. The key here is that clients are, again, required to follow your model—being paperless and using the system you designed.

3. Finally, suppose your client travels to an out-of-state vacation home. While away, this client needs access to W-2 and tax returns for the prior two years. If staff has to pull paper files from your office to fulfill the client's request, does this meet your collaborative requirement? Of course it doesn't. Again, implementing a cloud-based document management system that integrates with your broad technology infrastructure is required here. This will allow staff to simply upload documents to the client's portal for immediate online access by the client. The key here is having a process in place for adding specified documents to online client portals.

The second key concept is integration. As you build your ecosystem, you must ensure that applications integrate across the board to support the flow of data from one solution to the next. This offers extreme efficiency gains by eliminating multiple databases and re-keying data. There are two things to keep in mind as you consider integration:

1. Any solution within your ecosystem should not require an additional database. For example, having a database for practice management and another for tax only creates complexity, which is wasted time and effort inside your ecosystem. The goal is to establish a single database, which is only possible if your applications are seamlessly integrated. Creating a single contact database at Root & Associates was the single most important change we made to move the company forward in its evolution.

2. Any solution you use should enhance firm workflow, not add steps to it. For example, if you use or are considering a document management system that doesn't seamlessly integrate with your online client access and mobile solutions, you could be creating serious duplication of effort and workflow issues within your firm.

It's time now to apply the concepts of collaboration and integration to the applications within your model, including client-facing and back-office solutions. Let's begin by digging into the criteria used at Root & Associates to evaluate technology solutions:

Selection criteria for client-facing solutions. Make sure that you consider each criteria listed below as you evaluate different technologies, always considering the ability to support your collaboration and integration requirements. Ask yourself:

- Is the solution collaborative by design? In other words, can you and your clients access information in real time—anytime, anywhere, and from any device?

- Is the solution easy to use?

- Does the solution represent your brand in a positive way? (Note: the solution doesn't necessarily have to be branded to your firm, but it should be a positive representation of your brand.)

- Does the solution connect or integrate easily with other client-facing solutions used in your firm?

- Is the vendor stable, and does the vendor maintain a high level of security?

- How forward-looking is the vendor's technology, and does it match up with the way you want to serve your clients going forward?

Criteria for specific categories of client-facing solutions:

Client Accounting. QuickBooks and QuickBooks Online are the obvious solutions to handle work that is exchanged between you and your clients. If you choose a desktop version of any accounting software, you will need a hosting provider to support collaboration.

Paperless Document Management. To ensure maximum efficiency, it's important that your clients maintain digital files on their end and that you have access to these files. To accomplish this, you require an online document management application that integrates with the client accounting solution.

Client Portals. Portals are the common term used in the profession for technology that provides clients with online access to their financial documents. However, I elect to call this technology "Online Client Access." This level of technology is crucial on many levels. If you are preparing tax returns, financial statements, payroll, audits, or providing any other service, there's a good chance that you are using various software solutions to generate this information. For example, if you provide payroll and tax services to a client, your payroll software generates checks, W-2's, and payroll reports while your tax software generates the tax returns. Integrated online client access technology enables you to deliver all documents to the client seamlessly, no matter what application documents were created within.

Website and Mobile Apps. I will address website and mobile apps more in Chapter 9, but I think it's important to note here that it's a must to have your website and mobile apps integrated into your technology infrastructure. Today's clients demand online, mobile access, so make sure you can deliver—and that you deliver a rich experience.

Selection criteria for back-office solutions:

- Does the solution integrate seamlessly with other solutions in your system without requiring the addition of another database?

- Will the solution integrate tightly with other solutions in your system (both client-facing and back-office)?

- Does the solution allow access anytime, anywhere, and from any device?

- Is the vendor stable and established, so that you won't have to be concerned about the long-term viability of the solution?

- How forward-looking is the vendor's technology, and does it match up with the way you want to serve your clients going forward?

Criteria for specific categories of back-office solutions:

Practice Management. Every element of your back-office system should center on your practice management solution. This solution should serve as the "hub" for all demographic data, workflow management, time and billing, and firm benchmarking. Your practice management solution is the foundation for a single contact database, which is a mission-critical goal of every Next Generation Accounting Firm. I cannot express this point enough. Countless firms have experienced the chaos of dealing with multiple databases, which causes multiple data entry points, leads to duplication of work, and heightens risk of error.

Tax and Depreciation Your tax software should fully integrate with your practice management solution, so when data updates are made in your practice management solution, they automatically update in your tax software. Your depreciation solution should also seamlessly integrate with your tax solution to eliminate re-keying of information.

Accounting and Trial Balance. These systems should also fully integrate with your practice management and tax solutions. Additionally, you should consider a solution that will integrate with your client accounting solution on the client-facing side.

Document Management. The goal is to be paperless, so the document management solution you select is important. It should seamlessly integrate with both your back-office and client-facing online client access solution.

As you can see, you need to select solutions wisely. One low-efficiency workflow process in your ecosystem can wreak havoc on a firm. Think about how the infrastructure you choose will work for your staff, and remember that changing solutions is never easy.

As we close this chapter, I have a few final comments to share about implementing your Next Generation business model. Considering my own experiences and those of firm owners I work with from across the country, I've identified the two main barriers that hinder the ability to execute the vision and business model we've discussed thus far:

1. The inability to say NO to opportunities that do not fit your business model, and

2. The inability to make all necessary changes across the business to support the new business model.

In reference to barrier 1, continuing to accept any opportunity that comes through your door will most certainly stymie your transition. Perpetuating this approach only sustains a model of confusion. Conversely, once you begin to focus on clients and prospects that fit your business model, taking on those that don't fit becomes painfully obvious.

Here, I'd like to remind you of barrier 2, which I stated at the beginning of this chapter. You need to dedicate ample time to improving all areas of operation over the long term. The idea is to transition progressively, one change at a time, making room to successfully transition your business.

As we have discussed, the ultimate goal of the process that we are following is to have a firm with a finely tuned system and well-trained staff, only serving clients within your core competencies. Imagine if this was true for your firm today. Can you visualize the result?

Now that you have read about how to develop the right business model for your accounting firm, it's time to put what you have learned into practice and complete your vision. You have your end in mind, you know the services you want to offer and the type of clients you want to serve. You also understand the method you want to use to serve clients and the solutions to execute your business model.

While creating a vision for your firm is not easy, it is the starting point of your transition. Thinking through your vision and business model and getting it down on paper is absolutely essential in the transformation process. It's this work that will determine how successful you will be in implementing the remaining chapters of this book. Remember, your vision serves as your roadmap. Without it, you will continue to be unintentional about this extremely important part of your business.

On the following pages, you will find some worksheets and examples designed to help you through the process of "beginning with the end in mind." You will also find a copy of Root & Associates vision statement as an example. Take some time to systematically work through a few exercises designed to help you develop a vision statement that includes your business model. You'll want to have this recorded before you continue your journey in Chapter 4.

Next Generation Business Model Exercise: Creating Your Technology Delivery Model

Step 1: Write down all of the service offerings that your firm plans to make available. For each offering, identify the best way to deliver those services. Be clear and think in terms of end-to-end solutions, from point of initial contact to delivery and everything in between. Next, consider how you would use technology to make each service offering as efficient as possible, assuming that the technology exists (because it probably does).

Step 2: Using an application such as Microsoft Excel, create a workbook in which you list all of your clients in column A. You'll probably want to group your clients based on the type of service you provide for each one—for example, bookkeeping, write-up, payroll only, annual business and individual.

Using the technology solutions you selected for your business model (e.g., QuickBooks Online, hosted QuickBooks, portals), label the columns across the top. Label some of the remaining columns, out to the right, with the various solutions your clients are currently using. As an example, if your annual business client is currently providing you with a QuickBooks backup file each year, your ideal model says that you want your annual business clients in a collaborative environment (no backups). Place an X in your spreadsheet by the existing solution and fill the box with a color; create a new box next to this with your ideal solution. (*See example below.*)

The goal of this exercise is to create an inventory and to generate a snapshot of your existing clientele and the solutions they are currently using. Using the colored boxes, you will also get a clearer picture of how far off you are from your ideal business model.

Now that you have reached this point, you can begin implementing your system, meeting with clients, and transitioning them one at a time. At this point, you can start removing colored boxes and eliminating the X's—moving from where you are to where you want to be. This process takes lots of patience and tenacity.

Exercises

Service Delivery Worksheet

| Client Name | Existing Solutions | | | | | Future Business Model | | | |
	QB Backup	Paper Delivery	Paper Payroll	Paper Payables	QBO	Hosted QB	Portal Delivery	Digital Payroll	Paperless Payables
Annual Business Clients									
Client A	X	X		X					
Client B	X	X	X	X					
Client C	X	X	X	X					
Client D	X	X		X					
Client E	X	X		X					
Client F	X	X		X					

Analyze your current method of delivering services to each client, and create a plan to migrate service delivery to methods that enhance your operational efficiency.

Vision Statement Worksheet

Root & Associates Example Vision Statement

Our firm will provide outsourced CFO, accounting, payroll, and tax services to service-based businesses. We will utilize advanced technologies to support a real-time data-sharing delivery model and provide ultimate convenience for staff and clients. We will not accept clients that do not fit our defined core business model. We will provide individual income tax services to individuals that fit our defined return types. Our income tax service will also utilize technologies that allow our firm to deliver services in the most efficient manner. We highly value our firm's image, including overall office appearance and web presence and will strive to put our best foot forward with every interaction. We value life-work balance and consistently strive to maintain it.

Write your firm's vision statement here: _____

CHAPTER 4

Building Your Ideal Client Base

"That's been one of my mantras – focus and simplicity. Simple can be harder than complex: You have to work hard to get your thinking clean to make it simple. But it's worth it in the end because once you get there, you can move mountains."

– Steve Jobs

Do you wake up most mornings feeling energized and excited about your day, or do you dread the thought of what awaits when you arrive at the office? Whether you know it or not, a large part of what we do in our firms and how we feel about it is driven by our clients. As we discussed in the previous chapters, if the majority of your clients are dictating the workflow process or are not aligned with your areas of expertise, you will never be in full control of your own business. If this is how you operate today, it's time to get back in the driver's seat and take control.

In Chapter 2, you were asked to think about the type of clients you want to serve, primarily based on your firm's core competencies. Imagine how your firm would operate if all your clients were *ideal* clients—those that align with your areas of expertise and are served based on your business model's standardized procedures. Imagine also that you have a powerful brand that truly represents your firm and attracts the clients you desire. Wouldn't that be incredible?

I know from experience that building your ideal client base can become a reality. Back in 1997, my unintentional strategy to grow my firm was to take on whoever walked through the door. This is certainly not an ideal strategy. Consider an example within the medical niche. If you have a broken arm, you see an orthopedist. Why?

Because an orthopedist's area of specialization is congenital skeletal deformities. People with broken bones are, therefore, an orthopedist's ideal client, so they market to this segment and build their practice around it. Orthopedic doctors do not take patients with colds or sniffles (any patient who walks through the door) because these patients do not align with their area of expertise. The same concept holds true for an accounting practice.

Building your ideal client base is the change that will have the most impact on your firm. And that is why it's critical for you to do the work to identify your ideal clients. If you don't take the time to define the clients that fit your model, you will have no idea what they look like when they do walk through your door, or how to attract them.

While the wrong clients do generate revenue and help pay your bills, they ultimately cost you more via inefficient processes and tethering you to daily work. When clients don't fit your business model, they fall outside your standardized procedures. A feeling of chaos and insecurity about how to complete work pervades when everyone on the staff handles clients differently. All of this adds up to lost time and resources.

Inefficiency in workflow also affects your pricing model. If your staff is handling client work outside of uniform processes, it's difficult to determine how many hours it will take to complete projects. Being unable to estimate fees negates any ability to apply value pricing. The intentional firm bases fees on value and predictability, not hours, which is the only way to truly grow a business and fuel profitability.

Building a highly efficient technology infrastructure doesn't mesh well with the traditional take-anyone-who-walks-through-the-door approach. The chaos created by lack of standardization will only continue to be a drain on time and resources, negating many of the advances in efficiency gained through updated technology.

To truly transform your business and build an ideal client base, you must be on board to start saying "No" to clients that don't fit your model. Trust me; I understand that saying "No" isn't intuitive to most accountants. I can tell you from my own experience running Root &

Associates that turning clients away takes practice and commitment to the firm's defined vision. It was tough at first, but over time, I came to realize that I was able to grow my business much faster and more profitably by taking on fewer clients that were a good fit than taking on every client that came to us. Today, I'm running an organization where everyone on staff understands who our ideal clients are and how to serve them. This is one of the major reasons I have the freedom I do. Having a narrowly defined client base makes it much easier to train staff to be experts in serving defined niches.

Now, let's take a moment to recap where you are. At this point in the process:

- You've created a vision for the of type firm you want to operate.

- Your vision focuses on providing core-competency services to clients that fit your business model.

- Your procedure for delivering service is standardized, based on your systematic business model.

With these major milestones accomplished, you are ready to build your ideal client base. At this juncture in your journey, there are a few major requirements to fulfill:

Every new client that comes on board must fit the client type that you have defined and fit within your business model. New clients are exceptionally easy to add because they've been pre-qualified as a fit for your firm. These clients don't know any other way to work with you than the business model you've articulated, because you've set expectations up front. You are in control of the process.

You need to make a decision regarding existing clients that don't fit your new model. As you narrow your focus on your ideal client, you may identify legacy clients that no longer fit within your newly defined services, or who may be part of an industry that you no longer wish to serve. These are tough decisions to make, but if the client is no longer an ideal fit, you need to develop a plan for transitioning them over time.

You must move your existing client base to your new model. This re-training process is not easy and will take time, so make sure you are prepared and have a plan in place for this transition. The next section of this chapter will walk you through Root & Associates tested process for transitioning existing clients.

A How-To Guide for Transitioning Your Client Base

You may recall that at the end of Chapter 3, I asked you to create a technology delivery model to create a snapshot of your existing clientele and the solutions used to support them. This allows you to see how close or far off you are from your ideal model. While it does take some time to complete, fulfilling this exercise was a huge part of my firm's transformation. And I still use it today to keep track of where all our clients fall in our service delivery model.

When I started the transition of my own client base, I analyzed the client list within my technology delivery model spreadsheet and coded clients by type. Likely, these "types" mirror your own client base to a degree:

> **Low-hanging fruit**. These are the clients who trust your firm, are loyal, and will follow your lead without question. These clients will give you some early "wins" and boost your confidence as you proceed in your transition.

> **Need some convincing**. You will likely need to meet with these clients and ease them in. They require some education on your plan and an understanding of the value to them. With the right coaching, these clients will typically make the transition.

> **Will not move.** You will have clients who make it clear they are not going to make the transition with you. This is where you will be faced with a decision: do you continue to service

these clients or not? This decision will become more obvious as you transition your other clients and realize the burden of retaining clients that don't fit your business model.

Once I had completed my transition list, every Monday morning I met with my staff and assigned clients to individual employees. Staff members were responsible for assisting these clients in the transition to the new model. It took us about two years to move the entire client base. And yes, we lost some clients along the way, but, ultimately, the clients that left did not fit our model and needed to go.

Prior to starting this transition, it's also important to note that I took great strides to educate my staff on the firm's vision and the reason for the changes occurring. This proved incredibly valuable, because I had my team's support and buy-in from the start. I also had an informed staff to help lead our clients through the transition, all of which helped to accelerate the transition overall.

An Important Note: Specialize with Care

We have spent most of this chapter discussing how to build your ideal client base. And while part of this process involves clients that fit within your area of specialization, I would like you to take note of Tom's experience described in the book's forward.

Tom took great care to create a defined business model, serving clients within the estate and trust niche. While he grew his business based on this core competency, he was the only team member with the expertise required to serve this market. As a result, he is still working *in* his business—producing day-to-day client work. With Tom's experience in mind, understand that your ideal clients:

- Must be able to be served by members of your staff—not just you.

- Be part of an industry or service line that is large enough to provide significant and sustainable revenue for your firm. Serving very small niches or providing a standardized service that only a few clients need is not an efficient or profitable way to build your practice.

To close this chapter, the following are key steps to guide you in defining and building your ideal client base:

- Build your business model using the right technologies.

- Create your client inventory spreadsheet and develop your transition plan.

- Educate your staff on the details of your business model.

- Work with clients one at a time to move to your model, updating your spreadsheet every step of the way.

In the next chapter, we will turn our attention to the importance of identifying your unique abilities to have a greater, more positive impact on firm success.

CHAPTER 5

Identify What Makes You Unique – Then Apply Those Skills Accordingly

> *"Success is the maximum utilization of the ability that you have."*
>
> – *Zig Ziglar*

As a business owner, do you spend most of your day performing tasks that you are uniquely qualified to do? I'm talking about work associated with firm strategy—tasks that significantly and positively impact your firm and support your vision. Be honest with yourself here—is the better part of your day spent handling work that provides no real strategic value to the firm? I'm referring to such tasks as paying the firm's bills, invoicing clients, handling routine client requests, or even preparing basic tax returns.

My guess is that if you are like I was, you are probably handling at least a few of these low-value tasks…if not all of them. Take a moment to really think about it. If you journal out your day, how much of it is spent on work for which you are uniquely qualified—work that if you spent the majority of your day focused on would provide real value to you and your business—as opposed to just doing things that need to be done?

It's important to understand what your unique skills are. Do you know what makes you unique to your organization, and the work you perform that makes your business better, or do you just jump in and do it all? Trust me when I tell you that you do have a distinct skill set—one that can have a much greater impact than churning out tax returns and financial statements. Maybe one of your unique capabilities is analyzing your tax workflow, making tweaks to improve efficiency, and communicating these changes to staff for improved performance. Another skill might be networking with like-minded professionals and strategizing on building a better technology infrastructure to improve firm-wide operations. These are top level, unique skills that have great impact on your firm in terms of growth, profitability, and long-term sustainability.

Now, take a few minutes and make a list of at least six attributes that you consider your own unique skills. Think about the tasks that add true value to your personal and professional life and write them down.

Your day can be filled with mundane, routine work that simply needs to get done, or it can be filled with strategically driven work that can positively change the course of your business. The choice is yours.

I completely understand the mode of thinking that it's often easier to just complete a task yourself. That's how I thought for years… and that's what kept me in the role of technician. I handled so many routine tasks that I didn't have time to focus on strategic work. You have to change your mindset to start the transition from everyday tasks to progressively performing the work that requires your unique skills, the ones that will have the greatest impact. Think of the process as a continuum where your goal is to consistently minimize tasks that have little impact on your firm's broad success to make room for higher-level strategic work.

Identifying your unique skill set is a big part of moving you out of your technician role and freeing you from the long hours that come with it. It's about creating space to do more of the things that make you happy in life. This is truly where the rubber meets the road in your entrepreneurial evolution. So, if you consider the Intentional Accountant process so far—an intentional vision and business model, a sound branding and marketing strategy, and a powerful online and mobile presence—the transition from routine work to unique tasks is part of your evolution to becoming an intentional entrepreneur.

While I'm sure you are capable of fulfilling every job within your firm (and at one time or another, you probably have), these tasks are not what make you unique. To better emphasize the freedom that comes with this transition, allow me to describe my own personal transformation in this area.

There was a time when I paid all the bills for the firm and did the billing. I scheduled my own appointments, prepared the company payroll, managed employees, and even made sure the light bulbs were changed. On top of these tasks, I spent many days preparing client tax returns, reviewing returns for staff, preparing financial statements and tax projections, and more. I finally came to realize that just because I was capable of performing all these tasks, it didn't mean I *had* to handle them. I was robbing myself of hours and hours that I could have spent working on my business or with my family.

I finally came to the conclusion that something had to change. I knew that there would never be enough time to complete all of my technician work and still be able to transform my business. So, I began to think about what made me unique...the things that I *should* be working on. I asked myself: What are the tasks that, if I spent the majority of my time performing, would have the biggest impact on my business and personal life? I boiled it down to six key unique skills:

1. Strategizing on growth, profitability of service lines, and the right client mix.

2. Evaluating our business model and the ecosystem that supports it, and researching ways to improve our model, based on new technologies.

3. Creating content to educate and train staff on all changes.

4. Meeting with clients that have, or could have, a significant financial impact on the business.

5. Coaching my staff and helping them think through client and workflow issues.

6. Working to standardize processes firm wide to continually improve efficiency.

I have dedicated myself to following this list—to being true to my unique skill set. For example, I wrote this book during tax season. I could have spent my time preparing tax returns like I have for years. Instead, I trained my staff to handle this work, so I could create content that would have greater impact. I usually spend my time during early tax season evaluating our ecosystem and tweaking some of our systems and processes to ensure maximum productivity. I would have little time to do any of this if I bogged myself down with production work.

Take another example. One of my top-six skills includes evaluating my firm's technology ecosystem. When I spend time identifying areas in need of improvement and tweaking the system to operate more efficiently, it has a much larger impact on my business than if I were to personally prepare a tax return. Oversight of my firm's technology system includes tasks such as evaluating new collaborative accounting software, looking at ways to enhance our firm's mobile presence, and considering how to grow our practice with our ideal client types. If I kept myself in the weeds with day-to-day client work, client billing, and changing light bulbs, I would never have the time to perform the tasks that yield significant value to my firm and, ultimately, my life.

Your unique abilities will probably differ from mine—but you have your own set of skills, and it's time you got in touch with them.

Again, take the time to think through what your unique skills are, write them down, and start to make your transition from routine work to entrepreneurial initiatives that will have a major impact on you and your firm.

As your business evolves and grows, so will your responsibilities and the tasks you undertake. You must continue to ask yourself the question: What work should I be doing to make the biggest personal and financial impact on my business? My six items have evolved as my roles have changed over the years. Today, I continue to serve as President of Root & Associates, but I also serve as CEO of RootWorks. I now spend my time:

- Thinking about where I want each entity to be in the next three years. I'm constantly working on the strategic direction of both businesses to augment growth, improve the profitability of service lines, and develop my ideal client base.

- Evaluating our business model and the ecosystem that supports it. I'm always looking for ways to improve the business model, based on new technologies that enter the market.

- Creating content like this book, bylined articles, and white papers. Given my roles, I'm uniquely qualified to create content RootWorks, Root & Associates, and major trade publications—all focused on educating respective audiences.

- Meeting with clients that have, or could have, a significant financial impact on our organizations.

- Educating my staff and other practitioners. I put great effort into onsite staff education. I also facilitate up to 50 presentations each year at various professional events, impacting large groups of practitioners. In our organization, I'm uniquely qualified in this area.

- Coaching staff in many areas of firm operations. I help our staff think through client issues and workflow issues. I then work to create standardized processes that staff can follow with repetitive ease.

As you move forward, start to think about including time in your schedule for tasks that will have a tangible impact on your business.

Start by training one of your staff members to take responsibility for some of your administrative tasks. Then evaluate which production work could be handed over to qualified staff. Over time, you will start to feel the weight of day-to-day mundane tasks lifted from your shoulders and experience extra time that you can spend on unique work. I do want to note that chances are your responsibilities won't change overnight, so don't lose heart. It's a process that takes time. To create the "space" you need to transition your focus to more impactful work, first make a list of the tasks that consume your day. Include such items as:

- Answering emails

- Meeting with clients and prospects

- Assisting staff

- Paying firm bills

- Billing clients

- Scheduling appointments

- Performing client work (list out all client work: tax returns, financial statements, etc.)

- Setting up new clients

- Developing your online and mobile strategy

- Marketing

This list may be long, and I want you to be thorough and organized.

It's best to set up your list into two columns. The first column is reserved for tasks that require your unique skills, and the second column for tasks that do not impact broad change in your business— the day-to-day routine work. Once complete, this list should serve as a real eye-opener for you. If you're like me, you will be surprised at the length of your routine task list. This should be the impetus for delegating work. It's been my experience that practitioners who go through this exercise and actually do begin to delegate work get back 25 to 30 percent of their day relatively quickly.

If you are curious about where to start delegating, I'll share that I began with my receptionist/client service specialist. I knew that she had some availability, so I started training her to take over several administrative tasks. I began to immediately see space opening up on my calendar. Over time, my receptionist evolved into my full-time assistant, handling all my appointment scheduling and personal finances, travel planning, answering emails, setting up new clients, and overseeing client portals. We meet for 30 minutes a week to ensure she understands how to fulfill all tasks. This initial time investment has proven to be invaluable. A weekly 30-minute meeting ensures that she and I are on the same page—something that has significantly cut down on my internal communication. She is also well educated on my top priorities—my six unique skills—and protects me from work that falls outside of these areas. That means I have far more time to focus on work that will have a bigger impact on my firm.

A number of years ago, when my firm started growing significantly, I elevated my assistant's role to a full-time position and hired a new client service specialist to take over client service responsibilities, which were previously performed by my assistant. I also added an office manager to handle many day-to-day tasks, such as paying firm bills, handling client billing and collections, and overseeing staff and building management. My office manager also handles a fair amount of client bookkeeping work.

I've worked to build a team that can manage work that they're uniquely qualified to handle. At the same time, I've also been clear in communicating my role in the firm and the areas of the business in which I can be most effective. My employees understand that they are responsible for handling their work. And while I am here to coach and assist, I am to remain focused on the tasks associated with my role as the CEO.

If you want to move further down the entrepreneurial continuum, it's important to give up some of the habits that are keeping you in the role of technician. Create room in your schedule that will allow you to start doing the work for the greater good of your business.

Even with the right staff on board, protecting your time so you can focus on higher-level work is still a daily challenge. Just because you've made the decision to focus on bigger, more valuable opportunities doesn't mean that the routine tasks that have put a drain on your time for years won't continue to creep up. This means you must remain vigilant in reducing the time-intensive work that comes your way. The following are the most common challenges I face and how I handle them.

Challenge 1: Constant barrage of emails

Solution: My emails fit a few basic categories: spam, client requests, personal requests, and other business items. In Microsoft Outlook, I created a folder with my assistant's name. This is where I immediately move any email that does not require my attention. Spam emails go to her, and she unsubscribes me from many lists. Common client requests also go to her to handle. I do the same for personal and other business requests that she is trained to fulfill. I've seen about a 75 percent reduction in the amount of time I spend handling emails.

Challenge 2: Managing email expectations

Solution: My old tactic was to respond to email as soon as it hit my Inbox. By doing so, I set the expectation that I would respond immediately. This was a trap I set for myself. The fact is that you don't have to respond right away. Emails can wait. Change the expectation you've set with people by only responding to emails a few times a day, in scheduled chunks. This will minimize the constant interruptions that keep you from your strategic focus.

Challenge 3: Client work versus working on the business

Solution: While your goal is to significantly reduce the amount of client work you perform, you will likely never get out if it 100 percent. It's best to plan months in advance and block off time on your calendar to dedicate to client work versus working on your business. Your assistant will use blocked times as a road map to protect you from filling up your days with routine work. It's your calendar. Take control of it; don't let it control you.

Also be sure to delegate client work to staff qualified to do it. You have a staff for a reason; allow them to do the work for which they are qualified. In our firm, we generally have two types of clients: individual and business. For individuals, we do tax return and tax planning work. Clients that do not require my level of expertise are assigned to an experienced accountant to handle the work, start to finish. Each of our business clients is assigned a team depending on the services we perform for them; this includes an accountant to manage the relationship. We call this person a "client manager." The client manager is responsible for making sure all client work is completed accurately. Depending on the needs of the client, we might also assign a bookkeeper and a payroll processor, both of whom report to the client manager. I will get involved at a strategic level, but only as needed.

Challenge 4: Clients that expect you to do the work

Solution: For years I handled my clients personally. That set an expectation in the minds of clients, and rightly so. Break this trend by slowly transitioning your long-term clients over to a qualified staff member. Start by always having a staff member join you for client meetings, gradually transitioning your knowledge to staff and helping the client become comfortable with the new person. When I was ready to fully transition the client over, I set the appropriate expectations for follow-up with my staff and with the client. I make it a point to never go into a client or prospect meeting alone. By including a qualified staff person, I clearly set the expectation on who will be doing the work.

Challenge 5: Staff questions and inability to handle issues due to lack of training on technology

Solution: If your staff isn't properly trained and kept current on solution enhancements, you can spend hours helping them figure out technology issues. Technology does change rapidly, so when a new system is introduced into our eco-system, we have all appropriate staff trained. We also host bi-weekly lunch-and-learn sessions to update staff on solution changes and allow them to ask questions in an open forum.

As the leader in your business, there will always be demands on your time, but there are ways to reduce these demands and free yourself to concentrate on your areas of unique ability.

Handling these demands appropriately, as outlined in this chapter, will help pave your way to successful entrepreneurship and making impactful changes on your business and in your personal life.

CHAPTER 6

Building Your Ideal Staff...Getting the *Right* People on the Bus in the *Right* Seats

"The essence of competitiveness is liberated when we make people believe that what they think and do is important – and then get out of their way while they do it."

– Jack Welch

Many years ago, I had a conversation with a CPA friend of mine who was also located in Bloomington. It was the middle of tax season and he was telling me about his two-week getaway to Florida. Back then, I couldn't begin to imagine how he could swing this. I was working such long hours, a getaway seemed like an impossible dream. As I mentioned in Chapter 1, I knew there had to be a better way to manage my business, but I didn't know where to start. I asked my friend how he was able to leave during the most chaotic time of the year. His reply has always stuck with me: "Find good people, treat them well, and keep them for a long time."

A light bulb went off. I needed to build a team that I could trust to run the business and service our clients with the level of quality I expected—whether I was there or not.

To this point, I've talked a great deal about the importance of having a specific vision for your business and your life. Most entrepreneurs start their transformative journey by announcing "where" they are going, without regard to who is on their team. This can create some serious challenges. According to Jim Collins, author of the famed business book, *Good to Great*, those who lead their companies to greatness "…start not with *where*, but with *who*." In other words, they first work to get the right people on the bus and in the right seats (while also 'de-busing' the wrong people). Collins also advocates that great leaders must, "…stick with this discipline, first the people, then the direction, no matter how dire the circumstances."

Having lived through the process of building a great staff, I agree completely with Collins' assessment. There are few tasks during the life of this journey more critical to success than getting the right people on board and assigning them to the right positions.

To begin, you have to ask: "Do I have the right people on my team? Are they all assigned to the right roles?" In the previous chapter we focused on the importance of understanding your own unique abilities. The same is true for your staff. You can have the best group of people in the world, but if you are not helping them to maximize their talents and unique abilities, you won't get the results you desire.

I've certainly employed my fair share of the wrong people and had employees in the wrong seats over the years—something that made it virtually impossible to gain the freedom I desired. The biggest issue was that my firm lacked dedicated, structured systems and processes, and that made it virtually impossible to properly train and evaluate the people I hired. I never took the time to define positions and the qualifications necessary to fill them, which resulted in frequent turnover. This presented two major issues: 1) Having to terminate employees, which, no matter how well you handle it, will have a negative impact on existing staff. Good feelings typically don't come from watching your co-workers being let go and 2) There is a substantial amount of time, energy, and money that goes into training new staff. When employees only last a short while, you feel every bit of your wasted human and financial resources.

So, let's start with how you can avoid bringing the wrong people aboard. Let me first say, I'm not suggesting that I am an expert in human resources. What I bring to the table is decades of experience managing my firm and consistently enhancing our staff recruitment and retention system. I also know that at the heart of a successful business are the people. That said, the following is a list of initial guidelines to help you build your ideal staff.

Clearly understand and articulate your vision. I urge you to put your vision in writing so you know who you need on your bus to fulfill that vision. Yes, you need the right people on your team, but if your "end in mind" is not clear, it will be difficult to know who those people are. So based on your vision, what qualifications are critical per position—are you looking for employees who are technology savvy, self-motivated, organized, team players, accountable, detail-oriented? Think about the seats required to run your firm and the attributes of those who will fill those seats.

Take the time to clearly define and document your systems, processes, and technology. If you don't know what they are, you can't expect your staff to know either. Your employees shouldn't be expected to create their own processes. It's a terrible feeling when you have no idea what you are doing and try to do it anyway. Still, most firms lack the proper resources for training, do not have documented systems and processes in place, and do not have a standardized model for serving clients. The result, then, is that each client is handled differently and each employee adheres to his or her own process. Chaos. As business owners, we expect staff to be organized and function in a highly efficient manner; when they don't, we assume it's a problem with the employee and move on to the next person. This vicious cycle is hard to stop unless you take the time to define your internal systems.

Train staff appropriately. At Root & Associates, we have a mentoring system in place. Upon hire, every new employee spends a half-day with me. This allows for one-on-one time to articulate the firm's vision and expectations for the position. I educate new staff on the firm's ideal clients, business model, delivery system, technologies, and how all these elements fit together strategically within our broad system. This sets a positive tone up front and informs new staff that we have a plan, a system, and sound methods for execution. After meeting with me, I connect the new employee with a seasoned staffer who holds a similar position in the firm. This person is the designated mentor—a single point of contact for questions and training on firm processes and technologies. On average, this process extends 3 to 6 months.

Implement clearly defined goals and expectations. It's up to you to define goals and expectations for staff performance. This envelops all areas of operation: client services, unique role responsibilities, performance expectations, use of firm systems, dress code, and anything else that will aid in employee success. I find that it's also important to express the firm's views on hours vs. value. At Root & Associates, we bill based on the value of our services, not the number of hours worked. We apply this same mindset to our staff. We let our employees know that as long as the work is getting done and we are meeting revenue goals, we are far less concerned about the number of minutes they spend at their desks. This offers employees a level of freedom and flexibility that further elevates our positive culture. Flexibility in work schedule is also one of the most valued staff benefits we offer.

Be a resource to your team. I talk with many firm owners who tell me they're so bogged down with production work that they have no time to assist their staff. Like I stated in Chapter 3, these owners are "too busy driving to stop and get gas." When you make yourself unavailable to your staff, frustration levels will inevitably rise. Daily staff issues come up: uncertainties about how to perform an aspect of a job, challenges with technology, and so on. As the firm's leader, it's your job to maintain a level of confidence among staff—and that means helping them when needed. I make myself available regularly via scheduled staff meetings. At Root & Associates, we host a monthly lunch and learn meeting. This creates an open forum to update staff on recent technology additions and other changes. We also hold a weekly staff meeting designed to discuss client issues. These meetings address two key items: 1) They make me available to my staff on a regular basis and 2) They keep me involved with staff and apprised of potential client issues. Handling staff questions and issues at designated times leaves me free to plan my days and elevates my productivity.

Use incentives to keep your staff on track. At Root & Associates, we have a clear way of defining goals for staff. These goals help us to:

- Add to our highly efficient system.

- Provide outstanding client service.

- Are open to adopting and learning new technologies that improve firm performance.

- Embrace our team approach and spirit.

- Are committed to firm growth.

While a big part of making sure my staff meets these goals lies in selecting the right people in the first place, I also find that special incentives help. Most small firms, like mine, wish to increase profitability without growing into a large firm. Increasing profitability at a small firm requires the building and use of a highly efficient system—one that supports more work, in less time, with fewer people.

To foster continued revenue growth, without expanding our team significantly, I developed a bonus pool based on year-over-year revenue growth. The firm has a system for benchmarking individual staff goals, so at the end of each quarter, based on revenue growth, a percentage of profits are disbursed to staff accordingly. This has proven to be a successful motivator. It's also important to note here that you should include all staff in your bonus program. Your firm should adhere to a team approach, and rallying everyone on your team to perform will make a big difference in achieving your desired goals.

Until this point in the chapter, building your ideal staff has focused on your role as entrepreneur. I believe that the majority of employee problems are a direct result of leadership...or lack thereof. After identifying staff needs, getting the right people on your team is crucial. While each firm's structure differs slightly, I think most firms have similar staff requirements. The following sections break down Root & Associates staff organization and provide details on position qualifications.

Administrative

We support three administrative positions: personal assistant to the firm owner, client service specialist, and office manager. Depending on the size of your firm, you can consolidate or expand positions as needed. Consider each role within our administrative team:

> **Personal Assistant.** I consider this a very important position, and I've developed the role of this person carefully. Ultimately, this person should take a large chunk of routine tasks off of your plate so you can get back to working on strategic plans for your firm. My assistant's primary role is to shelter me from unneeded distractions, allowing me the space to work on projects that require my unique abilities. At one time, my personal assistant also handled all client service specialist tasks, but as my role in the firm expanded, so did hers. I moved her to my full-time assistant and created a new position for a client service specialist. I communicate with my assistant more than I do anyone else in the firm. She is intimately connected to the firm's vision and my needs as an entrepreneur, which helps her to fulfill her role with extreme efficiency. She handles my calendar, travel arrangements, emails, personal finances, new client setup across software solutions, and online client access setup for client-facing solutions. She also keeps me informed of any issues that arise in the firm. She is my gatekeeper—allowing me to function as a true leader.

> **Client Service Specialist.** This position functions as a "traffic controller," coordinating communication between our firm and our clients. Our client service specialist is the first person clients and prospects see and hear when they visit or call our office. As such, integral to her role is making everyone who communicates with our office feel welcome. From a technical perspective, she is responsible for client communications in relation to completed projects and assuring timely delivery of work. To be successful in this role, it's important that she is plugged in to all aspects of the firm—from staff roles and

skill sets to client project status and workflow processes. This ensures that clients are connected with the right staff member every time they contact the office. Additionally, the client service specialist is responsible for daily administrative tasks, such as scheduling staff appointments, managing digital faxes, handling in- and out-going mail, and practical execution of the firm's annual marketing communication plan (discussed in detail in Chapter 10). It is imperative to have an experienced administrative professional in this role who is intimately familiar with the inner workings of your firm.

Office Manager. Our office manager is responsible for internal firm accounting and office maintenance. This person handles paying bills, preparing payroll, making deposits, and following up on accounts receivable for the firm. Other tasks include facilitating building maintenance, holiday party planning, employee reviews (along with a partner), vacation scheduling, and handling internal staff requests and issues.

At Root & Associates, we've developed an administrative team that handles virtually all of the firm's day-to-day routine tasks. Again, depending on the size of your firm, you may consolidate roles. It's always been my strategy to minimize the amount of administrative staff in order to maximize revenue-generating staff positions. The central message here, however, is to ensure that you're not the one doing this work.

Para-Professional

Para-professionals are the backbone of my firm. Candidates for these types of positions, such as bookkeeper or payroll specialist, possess outstanding organizational skills, are technology adept, and have rudimentary finance knowledge. I've had great success filling these positions with former bank employees. These candidates tend to be well-trained, understand financial concepts, and have great attention to detail. Para-professionals, like administrative staff, will help to further remove you from daily routine tasks. It's important to create services in your firm that can be performed by para-professionals, because these offerings generate revenue that will ease the production burden on you and your professional staff. Consider using para-professionals to handle such services as payroll preparation, payroll tax returns, bookkeeping, and reconciliations.

Professional Staff

Professional staff may be the easiest for you to relate to, as their skill sets are likely closest to yours. These individuals must possess the right skill set to handle all client needs with minimal guidance from you. Candidates will have a solid understanding of tax and accounting, are self-motivated, and are dedicated to superior client service. I think it's important to also note that the new generation of accounting professionals want to work for a firm that is not only successful, but one that embraces new technologies, practices, and a flexible work schedule paradigm. There are a lot of talented people in our profession who are drawn to the benefit of year-round work-life balance, over the culture of a traditional accounting firm. Today's professionals are looking for a fun, innovative place to work with competitive pay. They want to work in a beautiful, modern office that offers standardized processes and a highly advanced technology platform. Being a Next Generation Accounting Firm positions you to attract these savvy, best-of-breed candidates.

Partners

I don't feel a need to get into detail about partner selection; the key here is to choose wisely. My current partner served as a junior professional for years, growing with the firm. In my opinion, homegrown partners are ideal because they have helped build the business and understand every aspect of firm operations. They also share your vision. My partner in Root & Associates oversees day-to-day firm operations, ensuring that work is delivered accurately and on time. And because he handles this aspect of the business, it allows me to focus on technology, business model, and all of the other areas within my entrepreneur role.

Another key to building the right staff is to keep your ears open. That means always being aware of people you come in contact with in your community who may one day be a good fit for your firm. This also means taking referrals from colleagues, peers, and staff seriously to keep the door open to those who may turn out to be a tremendous asset to your firm and enhance your team.

The Right Staff and Your Client Service Model

I've given you a clear outline for staff structure, complete with the core responsibilities of each position. This serves as the foundation for getting the right people on your team. The remainder of this chapter is dedicated to discussing how to align staff to support a strong client service model.

At Root & Associates, we follow a standardized model for client service. Depending on the type of client (business or individual) and the services offered, we match the right staff with the client to ensure superior service.

> **For business clients**. We assign each business client to a client service team, based on the services to be delivered. At minimum, a professional staff member is assigned to handle the account. Business clients for whom we provide our full-scale accounting services package are assigned a team—typically composed of a professional staff member, who serves as the client manager, and one to two para-professional staff members as needed.

> **For individual clients**. We assign at least one professional staff person, possibly two, depending upon the expertise required. If we assign two, one is typically a preparer and the other a reviewer.

At this point in your journey, a lot of the heavy lifting should be complete: vision, business model, technology infrastructure.

At this stage, you will have your system and processes in place to attract and hire the right people to get on your bus. You will have also made the necessary changes to weed out the wrong people who were already seated on your bus. Once you start to pick up speed with your transformation, there are those who will adapt and hold on, and others who will resist and depart. A friend once likened this to a merry-go-round: once it starts going, you either hold on tight or fly off. Some of your employees will fly off once you pick up speed, but likely that means they weren't a good fit in the first place.

Managing Change Effectively

This leads us to the discussion of managing change in your organization. Change is a constant in our profession, which means that managing change must be a core objective. It's been my experience that change is usually painful in an accounting firm. However, if change is managed properly, you can mitigate any negative impact. Following is our standard model for change management:

- Identify the change to be made; summarize why the change is required and the benefits to your organization.

- Define what the project will look like when completed. Also, clearly define project success factors.

- Appoint a champion who you trust to manage the project and deliver on execution.

- Test, refine, and then retest with a small sample size. Once comfortable with the change, implement full-scale.

- Offer appropriate staff training prior to full implementation.

- Implement the change fully.

- Hold regular staff meetings (weekly or bi-weekly) with your team to monitor successes and failures.

- Implement a way that staff can get problems resolved during initial phases of project launch.

Proper upfront planning is a necessity before you can move forward with any change in your firm. Lessen your pain by ensuring that you and your staff are prepared.

What I want you to take from this chapter, primarily, is the critical nature of having the right staff on board. Your ideal staff should include individuals that support your vision, have the necessary skills for the job, and are positioned to apply their unique abilities. The right staff is at the heart of a well-run firm. Without my team, I would most certainly be stuck in the role of technician and tethered to my desk. Having built a great team, my firm runs smoothly whether I am in the office or not—and that's where you want to be.

CHAPTER 7

The Importance of Planning to Get the Results You Want

"If I had eight hours to chop down a tree I would spend six hours sharpening my axe."

– Abraham Lincoln

This chapter offers the guidance required to properly plan your transformation from a traditional accounting firm to a Next Generation Accounting Firm. It's the glue that holds the entire process together and will ensure that your next generation evolution continues smoothly. Planning—methodical, dedicated planning—is at the center of your entire transition.

As you move forward to apply the concepts in this book, it's this chapter that will guide you on how to get things done by planning accordingly. As we dive in to planning, there are two items to keep in mind:

> **1. Planning is not a singular event**. Regularly scheduled planning is required to keep you moving forward.

> **2. Accountability** within the planning process is crucial.

I bring up these points because many plans start with good intentions, only to fail on follow-through. I've worked with numerous firms that begin the strategic planning process with excitement. They even implement a few, if not all, initial changes. Then life hits: emails, appointments, kids' activities, tax season…and these good-intentioned practitioners fall back into old habits. I recommend regular, scheduled planning meetings away from the office to help stay accountable to the vision and plan.

To make sure I stay on schedule and that planning remains a core element of my overall model, I attend a quarterly planning event in Toronto. At this event, I meet with like-minded entrepreneurs to learn, exchange ideas, and check in on my status. It's one of the best things I can do to stay on track. If I didn't commit to this regular routine, my travel schedule, tax season, and the myriad of other activities that fill my work and personal life would eventually steer me off course.

Up to this point, I haven't spent much time discussing my other business, RootWorks. I want to provide you with some context here as it relates to the topic of planning. I started RootWorks in 2007 with Wade Schultz, a creative and branding genius, and Ryan Deckard, who is also my partner in Root & Associates. Our goal with this business, from the beginning, was to be the primary resource for accounting professionals who desired to break out of the technician role and build highly successful businesses. This goal is encapsulated in our tagline: "Empowering Bean Counters to Become Better Entrepreneurs." We started RootWorks because we identified a huge need in the profession—a need for structured, dedicated education and coaching on building a business model, planning, technology infrastructure, branding, marketing, building an online presence, and all of the other elements that firm owners and partners are challenged with as they build their Next Generation Accounting Firm.

When we began working with other accounting firms, we were asked over and over again by firm owners: "Do you have a roadmap that I can follow?"

Practitioners understood the power of the Next Generation Accounting Firm concept and were eager to move forward. Essentially, they wanted to mimic many of the concepts we had accomplished in Root & Associates; they wanted a *view* into my firm. Over time, we developed a 170-step roadmap to walk our member firms through the process. In addition to this roadmap, we also drove home the immense importance of planning—just as I plan to do in this chapter.

A roadmap is simply that—a guide that plots your course. But simply having a roadmap in hand doesn't ensure that you will take the action required to implement all needed changes and make your next generation transformation. What I've found from working with hundreds of firms over the years is that prioritizing your roadmap and staying on track is the hard part. Planning and accountability are two key components in moving your firm forward, which is why I developed the "RootWorks Planning System." This system is designed to keep you moving forward systematically over time to ensure that you accomplish the items on your roadmap and, ultimately, achieve Next Generation Accounting Firm status.

The remainder of this chapter will walk you through the RootWorks Planning System. This system is composed of seven core components. There is nothing overly complicated about the RootWorks Planning System; it's really more about maintaining consistency and accountability.

The following are the seven RootWorks Planning System concepts that we will cover:

- Stay connected to your vision and business model.

- Stay connected to your unique abilities.

- Conduct quarterly assessments of your firm's progress toward Next Generation Accounting Firm status.

- Review prior quarter successes and set next quarter's goals.

- Review and evaluate new projects for future quarters. Create a quarterly game plan based on new project reviews.

- Create an implementation plan to ensure successful project completion.

It's important to house this information in a central location where you can organize your notes as you move along your continuum. I compile my notes in a leather binder that I keep with me most of the time. I find it helpful to jot down ideas that come to mind, including areas of my firm in need of enhancement. It's also nice to review sections when I have a question about what I need to do.

Now, let's discuss each of the seven system concepts:

Section 1 – Stay connected to your vision and business model

This is a summary of the work you did in Chapters 2 and 3. Your vision should be recorded in writing. A successful vision statement can be one page or several pages—the goal is to capture and stay connected to the goals you have for your firm and your life. Having your vision recorded and accessible in the binder offers a constant reminder of your plotted direction. The goal is to connect with your vision each quarter as you continue planning. Too often, vision statements are created and eventually filed away in a drawer—never to be looked at again. My personal goal is to connect with my vision statement on a regular basis, and that means keeping it readily handy, so it's not in the back of the drawer. Revisiting my vision helps to ensure that I stay on track with the goals set forth in my vision statement. It keeps me accountable and focused.

Section 2 – Stay connected to your unique abilities

As discussed in Chapter 5, honing in on your unique skills is crucial to your transformation. The goal is to get out from under routine administrative tasks and focus on strategic work that has the biggest impact on firm growth and prosperity. You were also tasked with creating a list of routine tasks vs. work associated with your unique abilities. The goal is to systematically drop routine tasks over time, opening up the space required to work on your business. Part of your quarterly planning should be to adhere to this objective. You will chart your progress as you move forward and continue to set new goals for getting out from under administrative work. This is where accountability comes in. I also suggest working with an organized group of like-minded entrepreneurs, serving as a built-in support group of peers who are all on a similarly charted course toward entrepreneurship. In RootWorks, we host quarterly meetings for our member firms to help ensure that everyone has the resources they need to succeed in their transformation.

Section 3 – Conduct quarterly assessments of your firm's progress toward Next Generation Accounting Firm status

This is the "roadmap" I mentioned earlier in this chapter. You can choose to create your own roadmap or use the one developed within RootWorks. Either way, your roadmap is a critical part of staying on course. Without one, you never really know where you are in the process, and that means it's difficult to plan future change. My roadmap encompasses all aspects of a firm, including such items as practice management, new client setup, branding and marketing, website and mobile, client accounting online, paperless tax workflow, a client service strategy, and more. A sound roadmap allows you to move forward with purpose and gives you the confidence that you are heading in the right direction.

I also want to mention that it's important that change not occur all at once, but is planned and executed over time. A solid roadmap will help guide you one step at a time to ensure consistent progress and safeguard you from becoming overwhelmed and discouraged. This approach allows for ample time to evaluate changes and celebrate successes along the way, which serves to provide the encouragement and confidence required to keep you on track.

Section 4 – Review prior quarter successes and set next quarter's goals

The goal of this section is to review your prior quarter and plan your next. Often we don't take the time to celebrate our successes; we move on to the next project without realizing our accomplishments. As you make your journey to a Next Generation Accounting Firm, it's important to note your progress along the way. Celebrating your successes will bolster your confidence as you progress—while identifying areas for improvement will allow you to make adjustments before they become major issues that may blockade progress. A good friend once told me that "…we may stumble a bit along the way, but as long as we keep falling forward, we can still look back and see our progress." This is not to say that you will stumble along the way; I just want you to understand that the goal is to continually move forward, no matter what's on the path ahead. Section 4 is about taking stock of accomplishments, changes, and lessons learned. It's smart to benchmark your progress in 90-day increments because it offers a panoramic view of your work, which makes it easier to pinpoint areas for enhancement as you plan for the coming quarter.

To fulfill the goal of Section 4, you'll start by reviewing your prior quarter accomplishments, noting goals that were successfully completed and those that were not. This is the time to decide whether the items you didn't accomplish are still important. If they are, they may be the first items listed for the coming quarter. As you evaluate your goals for the next 90 days, use your roadmap in Section 3 to identify the next most important strategic projects. Remember to review the list you created in Section 2—the list of items you should be personally working on versus those you should delegate to qualified staff members. Evaluate your list of potential project options carefully and make sure that you select the items that can have the biggest possible impact on you and your business.

Section 5 – Review and evaluate new projects for future quarters

In Section 4, you made a list of important projects that, when completed, should have a significant impact on your business and your life. In this section, our goal is to evaluate and gain clarity on each project's key success factors. Gauging the success of projects will help you assign a "success ranking" and the "worthiness" of projects, information that you will then communicate to your team. The idea of ranking projects in terms of success is critical. Remember, just because you put a project on your list a few months ago doesn't mean it should stay on the list. I use a form created by RootWorks to evaluate each of my firm's projects. The following are the questions and components within this form, should you want to create your own:

- What are the goals for this project? What is it you really want to accomplish?

- What impact will this project have on you and/or the organization overall?

- What does success look like in relation to this project? Write a few sentences defining what a successful project looks like.

I advise you to also make a list of the success criteria in order to communicate effectively to staff. This list will also help you to evaluate the project once it's been completed.

Section 6 – Create a quarterly game plan based on new project reviews

This is where you take all of your data from Sections 4 and 5 and create your quarterly game plan. With thorough, upfront planning, you've identified the projects that may still need to move forward requiring continued work (Section 4) and your new projects (Section 5). For your quarterly plan, you will identify:

- Project start dates

- Individuals responsible for planning and executing each project

- Resources needed to properly execute within the projected time frame

It's also good practice to identify a project coordinator so the work doesn't fall to you. Review your quarterly game plan with your project coordinator and with your team. Make sure to clearly articulate the expectations of a properly executed plan and the key success factors that will be used to evaluate success. And, remember, your goal is to consistently move routine items off of your plate and on to qualified staff. This is not to say that some tasks won't remain in your control; they will. I personally like to keep myself integrated in the process to a degree; this helps me conduct quarterly evaluations with clarity.

Section 7 – Create an implementation plan to ensure successful project completion

While Section 7 may feel a bit redundant, there is a clear distinction between your work in Section 6 and that in Section 7. In Section 6, the goal is to create a *quarterly game plan*, complete with all vetted projects to be implemented, due dates, and assigned staff. What you create in Section 7 is your implementation plan. Your quarterly game plan houses all projects for the quarter; your implementation plan allows you to schedule the execution of projects in shorter increments. In my experience, monthly and weekly increments are more effective for implementation. I personally use a monthly plan, which I review in staff meetings to keep my team and myself on track. We meet every Monday morning, and my implementation plan is part of that meeting. Consistent review of the implementation plan ensures timely completion of projects and offers a regular status check for staff.

These are the core elements of the RootWorks Planning System in brief. There is certainly more detail I could offer, but the idea is to give you the bones to create your own system. And these seven elements are good bones. No matter how you devise your system, be sure to remember that consistency in planning and accountability are crucial to the formula.

When your next quarter rolls around, plan a day away from the office and take your binder. When situated in your "quiet space," away from distractions, be sure to:

- Review your vision to stay engaged with your long-term goals.

- Evaluate how you are spending the majority of your time. Is it on tasks that require your unique skills?

- Check your progress against your roadmap.

- Celebrate your recent successes and identify projects that will have the biggest positive impact on your firm.

- Evaluate the projects based on success criteria.

- Create your quarterly game plan, and then execute.

I've worked with hundreds of accounting firm leaders from across the country, and I can tell you that those who have been successful in transforming their firms are those that take planning seriously and are accountable for the results. Planning is a critical part of your entrepreneurial journey. I know you have many urgent to-dos on your calendar, and it's never easy to make room in your schedule for a day of planning every quarter. I have the same challenge. However, if you make the commitment by scheduling your quarterly planning meetings, you will be amazed at the difference it will make…it has for me.

CHAPTER 8

Your Brand...Why It *Really* Matters

"This is a very complicated world, it's a very noisy world. And we're not going to get the chance to get people to remember much about us. No company is. So we have to be really clear on what we want them to know about us."

— *Steve Jobs*

Your brand is important. Period.

Keep this in the back of your mind as you move through this chapter. Your brand is the sum of everything your firm *is*, and why people remember you—or easily forget you. So the question is, do you want to be known as that out-of-date accountant portrayed on television… the nerdy numbers guys with the pocket protector? Or do you want to be the innovative, creative, progressive firm that people want to do business with—a brand that attracts the right people and is positively memorable? I'm guessing the answer is the latter. And as a Next Generation Accounting Firm, you have to care about how people view your business. You have to understand why your brand really matters.

I'm not sure that many accountants really understand what "brand" actually means. I certainly didn't when I started transforming my firm. It's not as easy to measure as other aspects of building a business. When I set out to create a paperless tax workflow, for example, it was easy for me to determine when I'd accomplished it. I designed the system, put the technology in place, trained my staff, put the machinery in motion, and checked it off the list. But how do I know when I've built my brand? How do I know when I can check that off my list?

The answer is elusive, because it resides outside of your company. When I first began to grasp the concept of building my brand, I realized two important things: 1) My brand is how people feel and think about my business; and 2) My brand exists—whether I had something to do with it or not. Not unlike the "unintentional business model" discussed in Chapter 3, your business does have a brand presence. It does exist. But it's likely that it is also unintentional.

Consider the accounting profession for a moment. As a whole, we have a brand. For years, the broad media has portrayed accountants as boring bean counters, lacking of personality and unattached in terms of personal relationships. The sad part is, the film and TV industry didn't conjure this image up. They were merely playing off of the established brand of the broad profession. Even today, this image is attached to the profession to a degree—whether intended or not.

Now let's consider a few positive, powerful brand examples. For me, Apple is one of the most engaging brands out there. When I consider Apple, I think: quality products, aesthetically beautiful and professional, superior support, powerful advertising, and bold. Even though Apple products are more expensive than other technologies, my loyalty to the brand overrides price. It's about the value. This is the test of a great brand.

Starbucks is another one of my favorite brands. I patronize Starbucks every day. Not only do I go out of my way for the product, I'm always motivated to go inside to order rather than using the drivethrough, because I enjoy the overall experience. My expectations for that experience are consistently met, to the point where I'm motivated to get out of my car and enter the store to order, even on a frigid winter morning. Without the power of the brand behind it, Starbucks coffee would be just a cup of decent coffee. It reminds me of a quote from Philip Kotler of the Kellogg School of Management at Northwestern University: "If you're not a brand, you're just a commodity."

As an entrepreneur, I now know how important it is to tap into brand loyalty. Your vision, your business model, and your overall system are brought to life through your brand, which is why it is important to move from an unintentional brand to a well-planned brand building effort. Both Apple and Starbucks are clearly the result of intentional branding. These companies have put great thought into the feeling they want to evoke in consumers, and so should you.

Invariably, the question that follows is, "Okay, how do I do that?"

The Brand Defined

Let's tackle that question by first defining in very specific terms what your brand is. Here is a composite of several definitions widely accepted among academics in America's business schools:

Your brand is a perception that exists solely in the mind of the consumer, based on the sum total of every direct and indirect interaction with your business.

Reread this definition a few times, and process it; let it soak in. Now let's break it down in the following sections.

Your brand exists solely in the minds of consumers. In other words, your brand is a perception that results in disposition or attitude held by people toward your firm. Business thought leader and author Peter Drucker summed it up this way: "Your brand is what you own in the mind of the consumer." In other words, your brand is NOT merely a logo, a slogan, an advertisement, a website, or a sign in your office lobby. These are all important means of expressing the essence of your business to your clients and prospects, but your brand is the cumulative effect of all of these things and more at work within the minds of those clients and prospects.

Your brand is based on the sum total of every direct and indirect interaction with your business. If I asked you to recall your favorite uncle, what would come to mind? I'm willing to bet that it is more than just the image of his face. It might be the pickup truck he drove, the hat that he always wore, memories of fishing trips, the aroma of pipe tobacco, corny jokes, and maybe the $5 bills he slipped into your pocket at the end of every visit. Your recollection is based on all of the experiences you had with him.

The same is true of the image my business, my brand, projects in the minds of my clients and prospects. Their perceptions and opinions will be based on everything about our relationship—every interaction.

Here's a challenge: How many different ways can you identify how you interact with your clients and prospects? Make a list. Be exhaustive. Here are some to get you started:

- Advertisements in the local newspaper

- My office front and parking area

- The sign at my front door

- My logo

- My letterhead and business card

- My sponsorship of community events

- My work product and how it is presented

- My reception lobby—the décor and furnishings

- The way my receptionist greets visitors and answers the phone

- My website—how it looks aesthetically and how it functions

This is already a long list, and it is by no means complete. But you can see how every aspect of interacting with your clients and prospects contributes to shaping their perceptions of your business and creates an image of your brand. If your office front is rundown, if your carpet is shabby and worn, if your receptionist is indifferent and aloof, if your logo design and stationery are amateurish, it is to the detriment of your brand.

Your brand—the overarching feel of your business—has a direct impact on growth, attracting the right clients, and staff and client retention. So, let's get started building yours.

Get Started Building Your Intentional Brand

Like every other aspect of your Next Generation Accounting Firm, building your brand requires a plan. And in the case of brand building, it is a long-term plan. Rome wasn't built in a day, and neither will you be able to reshape perceptions and attitudes about your business overnight.

The best way to bring a plan together is to prioritize according to which efforts are most readily achievable and yield the greatest impact. In addition, there are some aspects of brand building that need to be done in the right order, because other aspects will, logically, build upon them. For example, before you have stationery printed, it's obvious that you'll need to have a logo designed.

If you are like most accountants, the creative spark and skills required to develop your brand aren't your strongest attribute. My first piece of advice is to engage branding and design professionals to guide you through this process. I was in the same situation, and I knew I needed to hire branding professionals when I was working to build the Root & Associates brand.

You stand to benefit greatly from the support and skills of an expert creative team. The cost of engaging professionals for these services can vary, but with some research and due diligence, you should be able to identify a solution that falls within your budget. Seek out referrals from other professional services firms in your network, and remember to consider freelance talent whose cost structures are often less burdensome than those of established firms. Whatever person or company you select, be certain that you spell out the costs and scope of work precisely in writing, including overrun contingencies and not-to-exceed limits.

There are many elements to consider when building your brand. The following are the core elements that I start with as I worked to build Root & Associates brand:

Logo. Let me be clear that a logo is *not* your brand. Rather, a logo is a visual representation of your brand and will become the signature of your business. Your logo should express your aesthetic and professionalism, which is why it is highly advisable to engage a professional for the design. Ideally, your logo should serve your firm for many years, so be sure to carefully consider these factors:

Color selection. Ask your designer to create a color palette inspired by the character of your business. Limit your colors to one or two; more than this will make it challenging to reproduce your logo in a variety of applications, from printed literature to embroidered apparel.

Symbols and imagery. Try to identify an image that is a unique representation of your firm. This is challenging for companies that provide professional services. Avoid obvious symbols, such as the dollar sign or off-the-shelf symbols that can be purchased from online stock art collections.

Theme, tagline, or slogan. Ideally, this is a brief, memorable statement about your unique abilities. For example, our Root & Associates tag line is, "Leading our clients through the next generation of change." This helps express our commitment to offering value to clients through a mastery of evolving technologies and financial strategies.

Printed materials. It's important to have professional-quality printed materials in stock. Even though most communication today is electronic, there's still a place for printed information. Accounting firms remain a face-to-face service, with client meetings and consultations. Having well-written, aesthetically pleasing, and consistent marketing literature, stationery, and other printed materials expresses a commitment to quality and professionalism. These materials will also instill confidence in your clients and prospects. Be sure your printed materials consistently express your brand image through signature colors, logo, and tagline.

Your website. Think of your website as the new "front door" to your firm—a place to conduct business and collaborate with clients and exchange information and documents. To achieve this level of functionality, you'll need to engage a competent web developer who is experienced in creating websites with secure user logins and data exchange capabilities. At Root & Associates, our website is anchored by a client center that serves as the central point of information exchange. This is where our clients can view documents, receive alerts, and work collaboratively with staff. Above all, our site is intuitive and easy to navigate. Your developer must also have a design staff capable of producing a site that is an accurate reflection of your brand identity, complete with your logo, signature colors, and other stylistic traits. Your website is a place to tell your story, so make sure that your content is unique. Tell visitors about your vision, your values, your team, the services at which you excel, and how you do it. Finally, people need to be able to find you online. Be sure your web developer has competency in optimizing your site to facilitate maximum search engine results. Ideally, you want to be in the first page of results for searches of accounting firms within your geographic territory. Look for a web developer who can offer a reasonably reliable solution without layering additional costs for sophisticated, labor-intensive search engine optimization.

The Client Center anchors our website and serves as a gateway for clients to collaborate and do business with us.

Your office. The appearance of your office, inside and out, is a critical component of your brand. Your office exterior and interior should reflect your overall aesthetic and sense of professionalism. When prospects and clients drive past your office, what message do they receive about your firm? Do they see polish and quality, or neglect and carelessness? Is the interior designed with an aesthetic that reinforces your brand image? Are the interior spaces designed around greeting and serving your clients? The following is a brief checklist for auditing the appearance of your office. Ask yourself:

- What impression does a client or prospect get when they drive past my office?

- Is my office clean and well-maintained?

- Is my exterior signage well-designed and displayed? Does it properly display my logo and brand identity?

- What feeling does a client or prospect get when they enter my office? Does the interior design reflect my brand?

- Is my conference room well designed for the client's or prospect's comfort? (At Root & Associates, our conference room is a place where clients can relax, complete with a single-cup coffeemaker; a mini-refrigerator stocked with water, soda, and juice; comfortable chairs; and a fireplace.).

- Is my conference room equipped with the latest technologies? (At Root & Associates, our conference room is equipped with wireless Internet and a large flat-screen display to project client work for easy review.)

Mobile applications. The ability to serve clients on their mobile devices is an essential component of a Next Generation Accounting Firm. Mobile technology has become pervasive, and clients want this level of convenience to assess their financial information, anytime, from anywhere. At Root & Associates, we offer our clients a firm-branded app to access their accounting information on the go—from the device of their choosing. This gives our clients yet another choice in how they access or request their personal financial information—phone, email, client center on our website, or the app.

Mobile is what clients are demanding. Consider these facts, which were compiled long before this book was printed:

- By 2011, manufacturers were shipping more smart phones than PCs. (Source: Canalys Research)

- Nearly two-thirds of Americans now use smart phones. (Source: Pew Research Center)

- Roughly three-quarters of small businesses use tablet devices for business purposes. (Source: AT&T Technology Poll)

If you haven't made the commitment to mobile technology, you're behind in the game. When you make the leap to mobile—and I hope you do soon—be sure that your user interface properly expresses your brand to mobile clients by displaying your logo, colors, and other stylistic elements of brand identity.

There you have the beginnings of building a brand—the basic punch list to get you started. There are countless details and many other points of interaction with your potential clients to consider over the long term, but the major items that I have listed here will get you off to a brisk start.

Living Your Brand

Having a brand is a bit like having a faith—there is nothing more essential to its effectiveness than living out its values on a daily basis.

You and your staff are disciples of your brand, in a manner of thinking. In every business, it's the people that are at the heart of success. Your people (staff) are one of the most important points of interaction with clients and prospects. Therefore, those who "live" your brand are a part of your overall brand building effort. As such, make sure that every member of your staff knows what your brand stands for. Articulate the mission, vision, and values of your firm and your brand in a simple document that you can share, and regularly review the values and attributes of your brand during staff meetings, training sessions, and other opportunities. In other words, live your brand.

How Do I Know When I'm Done Building My Brand?

There's a short answer to this question: Building your brand is an ongoing process; it never ceases. This is another way of saying that your brand is dynamic. It can change over time to address new concerns and reflect new ways of doing business.

Remember how the brown UPS trucks for more than 40 years wore a shield-shaped logo featuring a package tied with string? In 2003, UPS redefined its brand image by adopting a new shield without the package, signaling its emergence as not just a domestic parcel carrier, but as a technology-powered global logistics company. The point is that business is alive and changing, and so, therefore, are brands. Your process of building and refining your brand is ongoing.

We've covered a lot in this chapter, but when it comes to branding, there's a lot to tell. Clearly, branding is an area that takes time, thought—and above all, perseverance. But trust me, as someone who's gone through the process, all the effort is well worth it. I have a brand that I am proud of, that is positive, and that was built with good and conscious intention. Now it's your turn. Start building your brand today.

CHAPTER 9

The "Front Door" *Redefined*... Getting Online and Going Mobile

"The Internet has been the most fundamental change of my lifetime and for hundreds of years."

— Rupert Murdoch

It's my observation that most accountants are very connected, personally, to their laptops, tablets, and smartphones—but I also know that, as a profession, we are trending behind other industries in terms of technology adoption. So why is it that practitioners don't extend this level of connectivity to their clients? This is a major disconnect in the profession. Just like you, clients are already equipped with mobile devices; they're armed and ready to be connected with your firm. Still, many practitioners have not bridged this connectivity gap.

Think about your own user habits, and consider the following 2013 statistics:

- 56 percent of American adults are now smartphone owners. (Source: Pew Internet & American Life Project, 2013)

- By the end of 2013, there were more mobile devices on earth than people. (Source: Cisco, 2013)

- 64 percent of affluent app users say they view brands with mobile apps more favorably. (Source: Luxury Institute, 2012)

- 57 percent of consumers will not recommend a business

with a poorly designed mobile site. Similarly, 40 percent of consumers will go to a competitor's site after a bad mobile experience. (Source: Compuware, 2012)

- 48 percent of users say that if they arrive on a business website that isn't working well on mobile, they take it as an indication of the business simply not caring. (Google Survey, 2013)

- 52 percent of users said they would be less likely to engage with a company if the mobile experience on their site was bad. (Google Survey, 2013)

The world's movement toward online business is undeniable, and each year the numbers are increasing. So then, the question for a Next Generation Accounting Firm is not whether you should have an online and mobile presence, but rather: What is your strategy to get there?

As I stated in Chapter 8, your firm's website is the new "front door" to your firm. This is where clients should go regularly to access their information and exchange data. Your mobile app extends the online convenience for clients by enabling them to access their financials on the go and from any device. The fact is, your clients will continue to increase the time they spend working from your website and mobile app—resulting in fewer requests for information via phone, email, or office visit. This is the level of convenience that you must deliver.

Building your online and mobile strategy is always easier if you have a few good examples to work from. I believe that a lot can be learned from the following examples: Chase Bank, Bank of America, Fidelity Investments, and Charles Schwab. Each of these financial service companies has outstanding web and mobile strategies in place. First, each has developed a website that is far more than simple marketing, but offers clients a place to do business—including paying bills, making deposits, and buying and selling investments. Second, each also offers an app that extends these capabilities to mobile devices. These examples are no longer the exception. This is the expected norm of the consumer market—and that includes accounting firm clients.

The big question is: How do we apply the strategies of these leading companies in our accounting firms? Let's start by examining some of their most important website components.

Creating a "hub" for doing business with clients (the new front door) requires:

- A designated space on the website (home page) to log in and access information.

- The ability to support transactions, such as bank transfers, making deposits, and viewing transaction history.

- A space to access static information, such as bank and investment statements.

- The ability to add functionality, such as new services, linking to other accounts, etc.

- A secure space to exchange information.

Creating an information space for clients and prospects requires an area of self-service, where clients and prospects can find answers to commonly asked questions or issues such as:

- A dedicated space for keeping apprised of interest rates on a week-to-week basis.

- Step-by-step instruction on how to open a new account.

- Information on branch office locations and hours of operation.

Creating a marketing hub for prospects and clients requires:

- Information on what differentiates the company from competitors—what makes them different, better, or special.

- A dedicated space for marketing promotions, such as free checking accounts, low interest loans, etc.

These are just a few of the key components included in industry-leading websites. Staying on top of these rapid changes to meet the needs of clients takes vigilance. That said, it's important to be flexible in your web and online strategy, so you are better equipped to implement change as technology evolves.

There are several template website services within the tax and accounting space that can support a few of the items mentioned in these lists. But these solutions tend to offer a cluttered look and do not offer the functionality to provide premium service. The goal of the Next Generation Accounting Firm is to create a highly useful, interactive solution that will support a rich client experience every time and that can expand as technologies evolve.

Now, let's apply what we learned from these financial-sector examples to your firm.

The question to be answered now is: What components need to be part of your website and mobile strategy?

Create a place to do business. Remember in Chapter 3, when we discussed the need for all of the components in your technology infrastructure to be collaborative by design? Your website is where all of these come together. Your client-facing solutions should all be accessible, within an organized, dedicated space on your home page. Likely, you have several different client solutions, so your website must be able to handle supporting all of them. Visit my firm's website at **Root.com** and review our Client Center. This is where we pull all client-facing solutions together for easy accessibility for clients. I will discuss this further in Chapter 11 when we delve into the client experience.

Create a space to offer useful client tools. Think through the operational pieces of your firm and the documents and tools required. The goal is to transform routine forms into tools on your website that make it easier to interact with clients and prospects. Consider operational tasks such as getting individual tax engagement letters signed, enabling payroll clients to easily add new employees or make changes to existing ones, and capturing a digital signature on a Consent to Release Information form. Then consider how to add these items to your website. It's these types of tools that will take your website from an online brochure to a practical tool. *(See the following pages for examples of tools available on my website, including online calculators, digital signatures, and electronic forms.)*

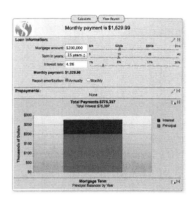

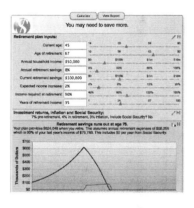

Give your clients and prospects useful tools. Our website features useful calculators that help our online visitors analyze their savings plan, mortgage amortization, financing strategies for major purchases, and more.

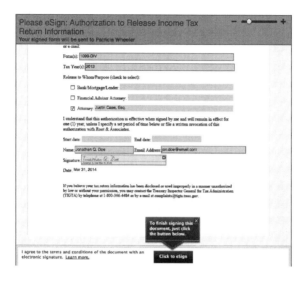

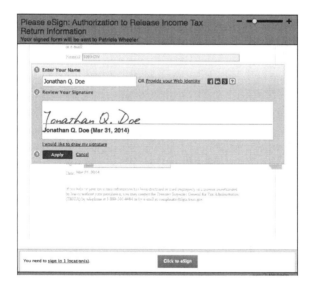

The ability to capture digital signatures will enhance the value of your website by enabling you to automate routine tasks, such as obtaining and filing consent forms.

root

EMPLOYEE UPDATE FORM

Date Submitted: _____

First Name _____ M.I._____ Last Name _____

Address _____

City _____ State _____ Zip _____ County _____

SSN _____ DOB _____

E-Mail _____

Marital Status: ☐ Married ☐ Single   Gender: ☐ Male ☐ Female

☐ **Hire** Date:_____
☐ **Termination** Date:_____
☐ **Change** Date: _____

Auth. Signature _____

LOCATION

Default Location _____ Other _____

Default Department _____ Other _____

PAYROLL ITEMS

PAY TYPE (*select one*): ☐ Salary ☐ Hourly

Salary: Annual Salary $_____

Hourly:	Rate Type _____	Rate Amount $ _____
	Rate Type _____	Rate Amount $ _____
	Rate Type _____	Rate Amount $ _____
	Rate Type _____	Rate Amount $ _____

DEDUCTION ITEMS

Pre-Tax Items:	Item Type _____	Item Amount $_____
	Item Type _____	Item Amount $_____
	Item Type _____	Item Amount $_____
	Item Type _____	Item Amount $_____
After-Tax Items:	Item Type _____	Item Amount $_____
	Item Type _____	Item Amount $_____
	Item Type _____	Item Amount $_____
	Item Type _____	Item Amount $_____

Retirement Plan Employer Match: ☐ Yes ☐ No   Match % _____

WITHHOLDING INFORMATION

W-4 FEDERAL

☐ Single ☐ Married

☐ Married withhold at Single rate

Total Allowances (Box 5)_____Additional w/h_____

WH-4 STATE

Personal Exemption (Line 5)_____

Dependent Exemption (Line 6)_____

Additional State w/h _____

DIRECT DEPOSIT

☐ Please attach voided check for each account (no deposit tickets)

☐ Please attach Direct Deposit Authorization form

NOTES

070713

Resources such as this downloadable employee update form will help clients follow procedures that streamline and standardize your operations.

Create a space to answer routine questions. Think through the most commonly asked questions that come up in your firm, such as: How much of my income can I contribute to my 401K? What are the tax brackets for married couples? What's the HSA limit this year? Instead of repeatedly answering these questions, create a self-serve area on your website where clients can find answers on their own and far more quickly than placing a call to your firm. This is also useful information for prospects.

Develop a space for timely, helpful information. Create a simple blog where you can place dynamic, changing content on a weekly or bi-weekly basis. Not only will this provide clients and prospects with current educational information, but the more relevant content you produce, the better your SEO (Search Engine Optimization).

Offer clear, concise information about your firm. In Chapter 4, we discussed the need to attract the right clients…your ideal clients. Your website offers prime real estate to articulate who you are, what you offer, and how you deliver your services. Take advantage of this to tell your story and set yourself up for bringing in the right clients from the start.

Develop a space to offer all client documents. Provide a single location to offer clients access to all necessary documents. Hopefully, you already store your clients' standard files, such as tax returns, tax source documents, financial statements, and payroll information digitally. Extend this convenience for clients and consider adding other documents for real-time access, such as insurance and disability policies, estate plans, real estate transactions, and appraisals. Enhance your role as the client's most trusted advisor by being a repository for all financial documents.

The world we live in today dictates that your online and mobile presence is incredibly important to the success of your firm. Don't take this process lightly and don't cut costs. You can't think of your website as an expense; but rather an investment in the long-term sustainability of your firm. That said, your website should be designed upfront to be flexible—built to easily incorporate new technologies as they become available. Your approach to creating a strong web and mobile presence must be dynamic.

The following are two good examples of how investing in a premium firm website have paid off for Root & Associates.

Example 1 – Client's employee turns future client

We offer full-service payroll, and as part of the service, we deliver all employee-based documents (e.g., paystubs, W-2's) to our clients' employees within their own secure online portals. That means that every day, we have hundreds of our clients' employees accessing our website and mobile app. One day I received a call from an ex-employee of a client. She had left the client's place of business to accept an office manager position at another physician's group in town. Her experience for years had been to receive paystubs and other documentation online. In her new role, she was picking up paychecks from her employer's accounting firm and manually getting signatures and handing out checks to employees. With her previous employer, a Root & Associates client, everything was offered conveniently online. She remembered this and called us to take over the group's bookkeeping, payroll, and tax. This has become a $25,000 per year client. This is where the value of a good online presence becomes overtly clear.

Example 2 – Online referrals

Within our practice management system, we track referrals closely. When we obtain a new client, we always ask why they decided to contact our firm. Frequently, the answer is: "I did a Google search; your site came up and I liked what I saw." We've tracked referrals from this source for several years and find that our average annual increase in recurring revenue from new business is about $80,000 per year. Now imagine this annual revenue stream over several years and, hopefully, you have a better understanding of the immense value of a powerful web presence.

A sophisticated and powerful web presence is an investment that must be made upfront and using professionals who know what they are doing. My accounting firm uses the team at RootWorks to build, maintain, and host our website, as do hundreds of accounting firms across the United States.

An Optimized Website and Mobile App

Your online presence is crucial, but lets take this a step further and discuss optimizing your website for mobile and a mobile application for your firm. Clients want access to information anytime, anywhere, and from any device. It's not enough to have a powerful website anymore—mobile is where the world lives, and you need to be there. Let me explain the difference between a website and one that is mobile-optimized:

A mobile-optimized website means that the site has been developed to run and display properly on mobile devices. Sites that are not optimized for mobile appear squished when viewed on a smartphone or tablet—a really big website appearing in a really small space. In today's mobile device-driven world, it's important that your website adapt to all devices. When your website is mobile optimized, it detects that it's being run on a mobile device and dynamically reformats to display information so that it's easy to read and navigate.

A mobile application is different than a mobile-optimized website. It is designed to augment your overall online presence. A properly designed mobile app offers a few distinct functions that make it easy for users to conduct transactions on the go. For example, a firm's mobile app may enable clients to take a picture of their tax documents with their smartphone and then submit images directly and securely to your firm. Additional functionality may allow clients' employees to access paycheck and W-2 information. The point here is to provide an app that offers added value beyond your web presence.

Overall, the purpose of this chapter is to get you moving on building a powerful online and mobile presence. Next Generation Accounting Firms are those that harness the power of the Internet to extend beyond onsite service and offer the ultimate in convenience through an interactive website and mobile apps. With the proper online and mobile strategy in place, you elevate yourself to the playing field of the big guys like Chase and Fidelity. And that's where you want to be.

Hopefully, you can see how all the pieces and parts come together. With a sound online and mobile strategy in place, you are ready to move on to the next chapter, where we discuss creating an intentional communications plan.

CHAPTER 10

Communicate with *Intention*… a Better Way to Think About Marketing

> *"The aim of marketing is to know and understand the customer so well the product or service fits him and sells itself."*
>
> – Peter Drucker

Before we get into the basics of building a communications plan and strategy—what many people call "marketing"—I want to be crystal clear on the order of how things should occur on your next generation journey. There is a time and place within your continuum to implement a communications plan, but this should not occur too early in the process, before you and your firm are ready. The last thing you want to do is launch a slew of marketing campaigns before you understand your vision and who you want to serve. If you are unclear in both of these areas, you can't begin to communicate effectively and support the business model that you will work so hard to develop. Like every other element in your journey, you must communicate with intention—and that means having all the right pieces in place to know what you need to say.

To clarify this point further, allow me to give you a real-world example. I recently spoke with a firm owner who was at the beginning of her journey. She was intent on marketing right away, before she had even developed her vision. She was clinging to the mindset that many firms at the beginning of this transition do: "We have to market immediately to build our client base and build revenue." And that's what she did. She took a shotgun approach to communications—blasting out generic marketing campaigns to a mass audience. While she did get leads in the door, they were not her ideal clients…and this only added more chaos to firm operations. Again, you have to "begin with the end in mind." Without a clear vision in place and without a sound business model developed, you can't begin to communicate effectively and attract the clientele that you desire.

With all this in mind, let's move on to a clear definition of marketing.

Marketing is Just Communicating with Intention

No doubt you've heard the term "marketing," and likely are somewhat confused by what this really means. Just to be clear, we will use this term interchangeably with "communicating" throughout this chapter, because marketing and communications are really the same. Every business has stories to tell about the unique solutions it can offer to solve the problems of clients and potential clients. Marketing is, essentially, a kind of storytelling and information-sharing about your business. Marketing is simply about communicating with your clients and prospects. I know that starting to think about marketing in this way helped significantly demystify the concept for me, simply based on how I thought about it and defined it.

When I became intentional with my marketing efforts, I still didn't completely understand the concept. After all, I thought I had been marketing my firm all along. I attended networking events, sat on United Way and hospital boards, and was active in my community. All of this brought in referrals and new leads—a core goal of marketing efforts, right? What I didn't understand is that this was only a small piece of a much larger marketing pie. There was so much more I had to learn.

Getting Started with Marketing (Communicating with Intention)

Marketing can be a scary concept to accountants, simply because it doesn't tend to fall within our typical core competencies. However, after years of running my firm, there came a time that I felt I had to enhance my marketing communications program. As I looked around at my competitors, I observed that everyone was sharing the same marketing messages: "superior accounting services...the best client service...the most reliable." Worse yet, our companies all looked the same, using template websites, boilerplate content, and printed materials that were less than professional-grade quality. In order to differentiate my firm from the sea of sameness, I moved forward in developing a sound marketing communications program.

What I learned was that a good marketing plan includes both my existing clients and prospects.

One of the biggest misconceptions in the profession is that marketing is all about getting new clients. While marketing to prospects is important to keep your lead pool full, it's critical to market to your existing clientele as well. At the core of marketing is nurturing client relationships by repeatedly hitting a targeted group with your unique message until they take action—call your firm, visit your website, and eventually sign up for your services. With existing clients, you've already established a relationship; they know you as a trusted source. Think about all of the opportunities to sell clients on added services. Most practitioners don't realize the gold mine of new business that is right in front of them.

In this chapter, we'll delve into many aspects of marketing, including identifying the core audiences to address in your plan and developing a starter marketing plan. While I understand that marketing lies well outside of the comfort zone of most accounting professionals, it is a necessary component of your business model. As I realized at a certain point, I could no longer ignore marketing and just "wing it" by being involved in the community. As with your business model, you must be intentional in your marketing communications; it's in your power (and your obligation) to tell your firm's unique story and tell it well. No one else can to do it for you, and no one else knows your company as well as you do.

When I first started to build the marketing plan for Root & Associates, I found it much easier to think about marketing at three simple levels: Who, What, and How.

- "Who" is my audience: Who am I communicating to?

- "What" are my marketing materials: What materials do I need to communicate my message effectively?

- "How" is my delivery method: How do I get my marketing pieces in front of my audience?

It really is this simple, so let's keep moving forward.

Defining Your Audiences – Here Comes the Who

First, I want you to remember that marketing doesn't start and stop, but is an ongoing effort. If you think about marketing as communicating, the idea of "continuous" is much more palatable. You would never stop communicating with your clients and prospects altogether, right? In fact, the more you communicate helpful, useful information with your audiences, the stronger the relationships, and the more quickly you gain loyalty.

Defining your audiences is fairly simple. For my firm, I divide our marketing communications across three distinct audiences:

> **Existing clients, fully engaged.** These clients providing every bit of business they have to offer, and aren't in a position to deepen their engagements with you. Your intention here is to maintain that loyalty by keeping the relationship strong through regular communication. Keep these clients in the loop with general awareness messages, appreciation for their business, and reminders of approaching filing deadlines and other key "touch-points" communications. You should also consider providing this group with a premium client newsletter, complete with helpful high-level financial information. Keep these relationships nurtured, and cultivate their loyal, repeat business.

> **Existing clients with growth potential**. This group represents the most productive for your new business efforts. It's always easier to grow your business through existing clients that have a need for more of what you offer. You have a level of trust established, so there's a much lower threshold of resistance, and it will cost you far less in terms of time and

resources to deepen these existing engagements and increase the value of the relationships. Be proactive in determining which of your clients falls into this category by conducting regular assessments of their circumstances and analysis of how they can benefit from more of your services.

Prospects. These people could benefit from your services, but have no existing relationship with you, and they may not have a clearly formed opinion of your firm. It's possible that they might have engagements with other firms. This creates a significant amount of inertia, or resistance, that makes this a challenging group to convert into clients. However, you need to make them part of your overall plan for balanced growth. Motivation for any of them to become a client might take a long period of being favorably aware of your brand, coupled with a change in their circumstances that triggers a call to you. Think of your communication with this group as planting seeds that will germinate in the future, when the time and conditions are right. Plant the seeds, keep them watered, and some will eventually grow.

Now that you understand your three core audiences (your Who), let's discuss the core tools used to communicate effectively with each audience—your *What*. Let's also discuss starting your marketing plan, which will include *How* to deliver your communications.

Develop a Plan Around Your Three Core Groups

A marketing plan is key to get and keep the kind of clients you want to serve. Mapping out a logical communications plan is essential to ensuring your success. A written plan will help keep you accountable for executing initiatives. Keep in mind that your marketing communication efforts will incur expenses; that's simply a fact of doing business. You'll need to produce a variety of materials and devices to help you tell your story. To start, here are the core items and tools required in your marketing arsenal:

Printed literature. This can include brochures about your firm and your specialties; fact sheets (one-page overviews) for each of your service lines, and a basic set of business stationery (letterhead, business cards, envelopes, address labels, etc.). Some firms (Root & Associates included) also have a nice pocket folder on hand to organize various printed materials for presentation.

Keep a variety of printed literature on hand to inform prospective clients about your service offerings. Keep in touch with clients and prospects with regular newsletters in print and/or digital format. Examples shown here include a premium client newsletter/ magazine (top) and various fact sheets with information about our services.

Digital materials. Typically, this includes emails and other digital materials, such as an online newsletter. You'll want digital communications to weigh heavy in your marketing plan. This will defray the higher costs associated with printed

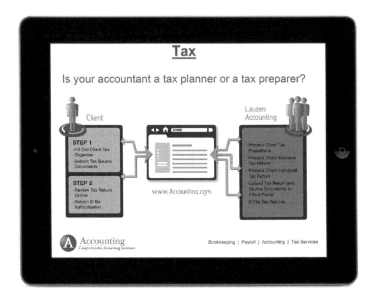

Electronic slide shows that can be displayed on projection and mobile devices are a must-have to tell your firm's story.

Website. This is by far the most complex and involved of your primary marketing tools, but it's critically important. Your website must be more than just an electronic brochure; it needs to be a front door to your firm—a place to conduct business with your clients. Your website is the primary call to action in marketing campaigns; that is, where you tell people to go to find more information on your firm. As such, your website must be highly professional and easy to navigate and contain all the information interested visitors seek. A capable web developer is essential in helping you with this item.

Your website should be more than an electronic brochure. Make it a place to do business with your clients. Think of it as the new front door to your firm.

Now let's put this all in a plan.

For my firm, I find it best to tackle marketing one quarter at a time. Start with an Excel spreadsheet and break it up into four quarters.

Within each quarter, make a section for each of your three audiences: 1) Existing clients, fully engaged, 2) Existing clients with growth potential, and 3) Prospects.

From here, fill in the types of communications (and the delivery method for each) that will go out to your respective audiences. It really can start out this simple. In fact, I've found this formula for marketing continues to work well in my firm...even several years into it.

With the basic format of your plan in place, let's start to fill in details. Within Q1, you have your three audiences represented (Who). Within each audience section, begin to record the types of communications to be sent (What) and the delivery method (How). I've included a sample section of Root & Associates marketing plan for Q1:

Q1				
Existing Clients				
Project	**Launch Date**	**Delivery Method**	**Status**	**Notes**
Client magazine	1/1/14	Print	Sent	Mail printed magazine to top 50 clients.
Client magazine	1/1/14	Email	Sent	Email digital version with announcement of new edition to all clients.
Quarterly Estimate Reminder	1/13/14	Email	Sent	Reminder to pay quarterly tax estimate due on 1/15/14.
Portal/Tax Organizer – Follow up Reminder	2/4/14	Email	Sent	Reminder to complete tax organizer available in the client portal. Contains portal instructions.
Existing Clients with Growth Potential				
Project	**Launch Date**	**Delivery Method**	**Status**	**Notes**
Client magazine	1/1/14	Print	Sent	Mail printed magazine to top 50 clients.
Client magazine	1/1/14	Email	Sent	Email digital version with announcement of new edition to all clients.
Quarterly Estimate Reminder	1/13/14	Email	Sent	Reminder to pay quarterly tax estimate due on 1/15/14.

Payroll Value-add Service Campaign	3/4/14	Email	In progress	Communication to upsell existing clients with payroll services.
Payroll Value-add Service Campaign – Follow up	3/18/14	Email	In progress	Communication to upsell existing clients with payroll services – follow up.

Prospect				
Project	**Launch Date**	**Delivery Method**	**Status**	**Notes**
Client magazine	1/1/14	Email	Sent	Email digital version to all prospects—with email customized for prospects.
Superhero Drip Email Campaign	1/7/14	Email	Sent	Email is part 1 of 12-part drip series.
Firm Introduction Campaign – Non-profit Niche	2/6/14	Mail	In progress	Mailing contains intro letter (on firm letterhead), non-profit niche fact sheet, #10 envelope.
Firm Introduction Campaign – Follow-up	2/20/14	Mail	Not started	Post card following up on full mailing sent (2/6). Call to action: download non-profit white paper from website.

Present at Chamber of Commerce – Small Business Event	3/7/14	Presentation/ Networking	Scheduled	Create educational presentation on better tax planning to mitigate tax burden for small businesses.
Present to Local Bank – SMB Loan Officer Group	3/20/14	Presentation/ Networking	Scheduled	Nurture bank relationship as main referral channel.

We've covered the basics of starting your marketing program. You know the Who, What, and How of a sound marketing plan. Just understanding the fundamentals of marketing, you are already several steps ahead of many firm owners. Now you just have to make it happen. It's time to execute.

Delegation is Key

I wouldn't be providing you with the full marketing picture if I didn't remind you to delegate.

As an entrepreneur, your focus is to work on your business more than working in your business. The tasks associated with marketing represent a set of responsibilities that should not be on your plate. While you may be integral to the marketing process during the launch phase, be sure that you identify a champion in your office who can handle daily marketing execution—a person to be accountable for the ongoing program. There are a few different ways to approach this:

> **Assign ownership of marketing activities to a staff member.** Keep in mind that, like you, your staff members aren't likely trained in marketing either. So be sure to make delegation a collaborative effort and provide plenty of support. Together, you'll not only be implementing quarterly plans, you'll be developing an entire approach for your firm to tackle marketing.

> **Recruit a college-level intern to coordinate marketing activities.** Seek out a capable, motivated student at a senior or graduate level to spend a few hours a week inside your firm planning and implementing marketing initiatives. Be sure you are able to commit to the level of supervision required, and provide plenty of direction, feedback, and support.

> **Engage a professional marketing firm or consultant.** This is an expeditious solution, but it can also be an expensive one. Evaluate potential business relationships carefully, and seek out referrals from trusted business associates. Try to identify a consultant who can help develop your internal staff to progressively take on more marketing-related duties. Have

an exit strategy to avoid incurring costs on a long-term basis. On the other hand, if an engagement provides a favorable return on investment, you may find that you're perfectly happy to continue the relationship.

Referral Channels Still Matter

I would be remiss not to mention referrals as a mission-critical element of your marketing program.

Referrals are a time-honored, proven tactic in our profession. A good referral program delegates some of the marketing legwork to your clients and other businesses as they send new business to your door. Despite the proliferation of new marketing tactics, identifying and nurturing referral relationships is still important.

Your best source of new business is still typically client referrals from referral partners. For example, at Root & Associates, we've developed strong relationships with local banks, which represent a strong referral channel for business leads. Many firms also ask their individual clients to provide referrals, mostly for tax returns. Some firms offer incentives, such as drawings for high-value items (e.g. an iPad or other technology product), or even small cash rewards for clients who refer new business. (Keep in mind that your state regulations may restrict certain types of promotions; be sure to consult your legal counsel.)

With all this in mind, take the time to develop a strategy to increase leads from your referral partners. Your efforts to cultivate your referral channels can deliver a highly favorable ROI.

Advanced Marketing Strategies

Once you have the basic marketing machinery up and running, you may want to explore some more sophisticated means of telling your firm's story.

These techniques demand that you have your core business well-organized and operationally humming. In other words, put first things first. Don't push the envelope with your marketing efforts if your attention is better spent on strengthening the core operations of your business. When the time is right, however, here are forward-thinking marketing strategies to consider:

Content Marketing—The New Paradigm

A revolution has taken place in the marketing world that corresponds with the abundance of information available online.

People in service industries like ours were once focused on keeping trade secrets well-guarded. The new approach of content marketing is "self-serve information." Research from Sirius Decisions shows that business-to-business customers have 70 percent of the purchase decision completed before they ever contact the company. This is true in our industry, too. Potential customers are "secret shopping" accountants, looking for services information, online reviews, and other digital cues about your value and expertise. Smart firms are not running away from this trend, but are instead running toward it by providing volumes of online information—tips and how-to's—that previously would have seemed unthinkable.

The information provided shouldn't be solely about your firm, either. That's just a brochure in a new guise. Instead, much of this information must be truly and inherently useful.

This concept of "offering information that is so useful, people will actually pay for it when asked," is derived from the New York Times best-selling business book *Youtility*, by Jay Baer. The book (and its companion eBook, *Youtility for Accountants*) shows that business success is all about helping, not marketing hype. Giving away valuable, educational resources and information is a way to break through the messaging clutter and client distrust to earn consumer trust and eventually convert them to clients.

Don't think for a moment, however, that Jay is simply encouraging us to be useful and helpful for its own sake. This isn't about earning a merit badge; it's about understanding the new realities at work in the marketplace—and specifically in the accounting profession. The idea here is to give away information snacks in order to sell knowledge meals down the road.

Here are some basic examples of how you can put content marketing to work for your firm:

Make useful information available for download on your website. The cost of downloading is simply a name and email address, which allows you to reach out and offer more help, in the form of information or an engagement. Content available for download could include documents such as annual tax planning guides, white papers explaining various aspects of the tax code, or other useful documents.

2014 Tax Guide

2014 Tax Guide

2014 Tax Guide

Our annual Tax Guide is a popular download and an excellent example of the Youtility marketing approach.

Write a blog. A blog is an online journal, hosted on your own website or another forum. Your blog can be used to communicate all kinds of helpful information—from approaching deadlines to insight on tax code changes, to general tips on financial management. Keep in mind that we need to be vigilant about information we share not being construed as advice. You'll always want to make appropriate disclaimers to stay within the bounds of what's acceptable within the confines of the law and our professional code of conduct.

Use your social media channels. Produce an educational video to post on YouTube. Use Twitter and Facebook status updates to remind your followers of important deadlines approaching or significant news regarding financial management. Or you can use these channels to comment on breaking news relevant to your clientele.

Host a brown-bag lunch event. Content marketing need not reside entirely online. Offer your time to meet with interested entrepreneurs and offer them some basic training in financial literacy. It's a good way to make new friends and cultivate high regard and goodwill among people in the business community.

Niche Marketing—Specialization

If you have an area of specialized professional expertise, and have solved the accounting puzzle for a specific industry or trade in a way that no one else has, you have an opportunity to develop a program of niche marketing.

Niche marketing is considered by many firms to be the Holy Grail— the ultimate destination in the marketing quest—because it defines a truly distinctive point of difference for your firm. It provides a unique position of ownership in a market segment. For example, if your firm has expertise in servicing veterinarian clinics, this is a group that you would target in your marketing program.

My own firm emphasizes independent service-based businesses, physicians, dentists, and law firms as its niche specialties. I have colleagues who have carved out niches in construction, government contracting, non-profits, and scores of other markets. Some of them have grown the scope of their practices and clientele from local to interstate as a result of their niche specializations. The rewards can be considerable, but remember that you need to build your competency. Even if you develop a niche specialty, you may wish to counterbalance that revenue stream with other market segments, so that your entire business isn't predicated on the success of a single industry. (Think about what the impact on your firm would've been in 2008-09 if you exclusively served homebuilders or real estate businesses, for example.)

Many owners follow the rule of thumb that no more than a third of your business should be tied to any one client or market segment. This still leaves a lot of room to develop a niche specialty.

What To Do When Your Marketing Works

It is important that once you have generated leads and referrals that you develop a standardized system for meeting with new prospects. This could include a friendly phone call from the staff member handling your marketing, inviting the prospect to the firm for a consultation. Once they're in the door, you or another partner can offer a professionally developed and engaging presentation that showcases your firm's value propositions and how you can help the prospect achieve their business goals. And once you secure new clients, you'll want to have a standardized system for ensuring a rich experience for them from the start.

Once you have implemented your marketing program, you will want to periodically evaluate the results. The ultimate measure of your success will, of course, be the number of new clients you have and additional business from existing clients, both of which will likely signal some changes for your firm.

I would like to end this chapter by advising you to be patient. Don't be discouraged by a slow start in any aspect of marketing. Marketing is a slow burn—not the kind of work you'll find exciting if you need instant gratification. People aren't going to beat a path to your door the instant they see one of your advertisements, postcards, or emails. The reward in marketing comes, rather, through persistence. Be persistent with clear intent, and tell your story to the right people.

CHAPTER 11

Ensuring a Rich Client Experience...Every Time

"I am concerned about any attrition in customer traffic at Starbucks, but I don't want to use the economy, commodity prices or consumer confidence as an excuse. We must maintain a value proposition to our customers as well as differentiate the Starbucks Experience. That is the key."

— Howard Schultz

At this point in the book, you should have a firm grasp on your vision, business model, and the need for a tightly integrated technology infrastructure. You also understand the necessity of a powerful brand and web presence, sound marketing, and planning. That's a lot to take in, but all essential elements of the big picture—and all crucial to the mission of ensuring a rich client experience...every time.

As we discussed in Chapter 8, your brand is a perception in the mind of the consumer based on the sum of all interactions with your business. And a core interaction includes the overall client experience. If your client service is poor, it will detract greatly from your brand. And in a business where service is at the heart of what we do, this is detrimental. So, understand that every interaction you have with clients and prospects becomes part of your brand image to ensure that you are known for superior service—the kind of service that promises the highest degree of client loyalty.

Consider the Ritz-Carlton as an example of superior service. When you think about the Ritz name, it's likely that your perception is positive. And if you've stayed at a Ritz-Carlton, I'm sure you'll agree that the hotel's top-level customer service is a big part of this. In fact, I've worked with the Ritz for years to plan RootWorks events, so I know firsthand how committed the company is to offering the richest client experience possible. This is more than evident in the company's credo:

> *"The Ritz-Carlton Hotel is a place where the genuine care and comfort of our guests is our highest mission. We pledge to provide the finest personal service and facilities for our guests who will always enjoy a warm, relaxed, yet refined ambience. The Ritz-Carlton experience enlivens the senses, instills well-being, and fulfills even the unexpressed wishes and needs of our guests."*

Clearly, the Ritz has a defined vision, and works to ensure that this vision is met with every client interaction. The Ritz-Carlton Hotel claims that the lifetime value of a new guest is $100,000, which is telling about how the company views its guests—as its richest investment. So, how does the Ritz ensure a superior experience every time? Let's dissect the client process a bit further:

The Ritz offers what it terms the "Three Steps of Service." This includes:

- Offering a warm, personal, and sincere greeting— addressing the guest by name.

- Anticipating and fulfilling each guest's needs.

- Offering a warm, personal, and sincere farewell— addressing the guest by name.

This approach is simple, yet its extremely effective. If we delve even deeper into a few of the Ritz's "Service Values," the company is steadfast in its commitment to:

- Continually build strong relationships with guests— for life.

- Be responsive to expressed and unexpressed needs.

- Work to create unique, memorable guest experiences.

- Continually seek opportunities to innovate and improve the customer experience.

Every part of the Ritz service mission is centered on the guest experience; the company has defined its vision and created a business model that ensures the vision is upheld at all times. From exceptional employee training to the hotel's pre-shift "daily line-up," where every employee undergoes a 15-minute review of the company's objectives and commitment to quality service, the Ritz-Carlton is vigilant about maintaining its mission and vision.

What would happen in your firm if serving clients was such a priority that you held regular staff meetings to discuss improving the client experience? It's likely that there are few competitor firms that take the client experience as seriously as the Ritz-Carlton. If your firm shifted to this model, how would that differentiate you further? I'll tell you from experience, if done right, it will elevate your firm to a level far above any other. Clients don't forget when they've been treated with superior service—and they tend to stay for the long term.

Have you ever considered the lifetime value of a new client—or an existing client, for that matter? Remember earlier that I stated the Ritz claims a $100,000 value on new guests. This can be exceeded in your firm. Consider a few examples:

- An annual Individual tax client at $500/year over 20 years = a lifetime value of $10,000.

- An annual small business tax client at $2,500/year over 20 years = a lifetime value of $50,000.

- A small business client that requires payroll, monthly accounting, and annual tax services at $750/ month = a lifetime value of $180,000.

- A full-service bookkeeping client that requires payroll, monthly accounting, annual tax services, and accounts payable support at $2,500/month = a lifetime value of $600,000.

These numbers offer a fresh new perspective on what client value really means. The key here is retaining clients in order to realize long-term value. And how do you keep your clients loyal? By offering them superior, above-and-beyond service without compromise.

As we discussed the unintentional brand in Chapter 8, each firm also offers a certain client experience—and my guess is that it's unintentional as well. It's possible that your client experience was established years ago and is running on autopilot. The problem with this model—the "if it ain't broke" theory—is that it negates any action on enriching the client experience. It bars firms from setting the standard for client service. And, trust me, if you are not setting the standard, one of your competitors certainly will. The Ritz-Carlton doesn't leave this foundational brand element to chance; the client experience is highly intentional, thoughtful, and fiercely adhered to.

A 2011 global study conducted by KRC Research, titled "Best Experience Brands," reported that brands that will lead in the 21st century are those that offer a powerful client experience. These are brands that will continue to invest in building and improving the consumer experience because they firmly believe that the client experience is a key point of differentiation and a main reason consumers become customers and advocates.

Some interesting data from the study includes:

- Consumers willing to pay a premium price for a product or service if they know they will have a unique experience with that brand: *94 percent agree or strongly agree.*

- Consumers who believe that the overall experience with a brand is the single biggest factor in deciding to purchase a product or a service: *95 percent agree or strongly agree.*

- Consumers who believe a previous unique experience is

very important in deciding what specific brands to use in the future: *62 percent strongly agree.*

This report indicates a clear trend in client expectations of service. The same is true for the accounting profession. To ensure your journey to Next Generation Accounting Firm status, the client experience is a critical pin in your roadmap. And that means you have to be intentional in terms of the service and the experience you provide every client, every time.

Before we delve into the four key components of client service that I've defined for my own firm, I want to clarify that part of an exceptional experience is also serving the client when and where they want to be served. Clients are online and they want access to their information and your services at their convenience—on a mobile device, in their office, from home, or any combination of these examples. The highest level of service is not always meeting in person with a client; if that's not the method the client values, then it won't be perceived as excellent service.

Also notice that I didn't mention how the client is served. There's a big difference in providing clients with the convenience and flexibility of accessing services 24/7 from the device of their choosing vs. opening the door to allowing the client to mandate how your services are delivered. Service delivery must always remain in the control of your firm, or the clients will follow the workflow of their choosing. This is what's gotten so many firms in trouble.

There are four key components that I've defined in my own firm to ensure a unique, rich experience for our clients.

Onsite. We work in a profession that, to a degree, still relies on in-person and over-the-phone communication. As a provider of professional services, it's our duty to work in partnership with our clients throughout the year…and that means meetings, informative conversations, and regular coaching to ensure the client's understanding of their data and financial health. That said, what does your office look like—inside and out? What perception comes to mind when you look at your building's façade or walk around from office to office? Is your property nicely landscaped? Is the interior well lit, comfortable, and elegantly decorated? Do you offer convenient and ample parking? Bottom line: your onsite presence should match your online brand—clean, well maintained, professional, convenient, and approachable?

Beyond the aesthetics of your office space, you also have to think through every aspect of a live-person interaction. Consider each interaction point and ensure that you are providing the richest client experience possible:

> **Office Visit.** When a client or prospect enters your office, they should feel immediately comfortable. Beyond a professional and warm office, ensure they are greeted and welcomed. The person covering reception is the first point of interaction, so make sure you have the right person in place to make a great first impression. Like at the Ritz-Carlton, this person should offer a warm greeting and use the client's name. This person should also anticipate the client's needs and have any documentation ready to hand over. A typical interaction at my firm is: ""Hi Sara [client's name]. I thought I saw you drive in; here's the information you requested, all ready for you." For a client meeting, the interaction changes: "Hi Sara. Welcome. Darren is expecting you. Let me show you to the conference room. We have our guest Wi-Fi network if you need it, and here's a card with access information. Can I get you something to drink? If you need anything, please let me know; I'm sitting right outside the conference room." Also be conscious of making the client wait too long. Be punctual. The richest client experience is in the details, so be intentional about every aspect of your client's experience with you and your staff.

> **Telephone Call.** Not all visits from clients are onsite. The phone is still a main vehicle of communication, so ensure that clients and prospects get the same level of curiosity and warmth when they call. When a client or prospect calls your office, they do not expect to get a digital recording. Dedicate a person or persons to cover the phones during the workday

to ensure that those calling in get personal, live attention. It's also a good idea to invest in hold music. It's a nice touch to offer soothing music when waiting to be transferred.

New Client and Prospect Process. Do you have a defined process for communicating with new clients and prospects? If not, you'll need one in place. No matter who answers the phone or is covering the front desk, new clients and prospect interactions should always be handled the same way. Have a protocol for assessing who should help based on the client's or prospect's needs. Also have ready-packaged information that you can offer new clients. At Root & Associates, we have a "New Client Welcome Kit," which includes an overview of firm services and a helpful team contact list.

Online and Mobile. Your website and mobile presence is an area where you need to invest both time and money, as your digital existence will set the stage for superior client service. We discussed your website as the "new front door" to your firm. It's a place for clients to do business and exchange information with your staff conveniently and without interruption. Your website needs to be state-of-the-art and provide online conveniences, such as portals, to set your firm apart. When working through your online presence, consider the following components:

- *Easy Password Management.* Offer clients the ability to self-manage their own password. Most of us have multiple passwords to remember these days. It's natural to forget a password now and again, so make sure your clients have the ability to reset their password immediately when needed.

- *Access to Documents.* Offer real-time access to client documents, displayed in a way that is most logical to your clients (not to your firm). For example, organize tax returns in a "Tax Return" folder and financial statements in a "Financial Statement" folder. The easier documents are to locate, the richer the client interaction. Find the right solution to create an online system where all documents are available under a single login for clients, from tax documents to payroll reports. There are several available in the marketplace.

- *Accounting System Access.* Offer simple, secure access to your collaborative client accounting applications directly from your website. Again, it's all about making it convenient for the client.

- *Access to Answers.* Make sure you fulfill your clients "unexpressed" needs. You know the most commonly asked questions from clients, so be proactive and develop a comprehensive Frequently Asked Questions section on your website. Offer clients a shortcut to the answers they regularly seek.

- *Added Convenience Options.* There are a number of ways you can augment the digital experience for clients. Consider adding the ability for clients to book appointments, pay invoices, check the status of their tax return, and upload tax source documents online. You can also add a feature that allows clients to request that documents be sent to a specific financial institution.

The key here is to always think about the experience from the client's perspective. How would my clients want to interact with my firm? Answer: quickly, easily, and securely.

Service Experience. You should be able to sum up your service experience in four words: timely, responsive, accurate, and friendly. Early in my career, I asked a friend why his law firm was so successful. His response was: "We always exceed expectations. Most law firms do not focus on timeliness; we do." It seems so simple: deliver services on time. However, many professionals fail miserably in this area. At Root & Associates, we've worked arduously over the years to ensure we always deliver in a timely manner. I've built my practice to be a highly efficient machine—in terms of technology infrastructure, standardized processes, building a best-of-breed staff, etc.—and this all supports timely delivery. With the right model and systems in place, your firm will also be better positioned to deliver on responsiveness, accuracy of product, and providing a rich client experience...every time.

Community Experience. How people view your business in the community is also a key point in terms of the larger client experience. There are a few key questions to ask: Is your firm a good corporate citizen, one that is seen giving back to the community? Are you or your staff involved in local charity events, perhaps serving on a local non-profit board? What you want to consider here is potential referral sources. The best referrals are from those that truly respect your firm and understand that you are an asset to the community.

There is a lot to absorb in this chapter, but I believe that every element of the client experience is critical. Every interaction you have with clients and prospects builds on the perception they have about your business—so you don't want to leave anything to chance. Don't run your practice unintentionally. Take charge of your client experience; make it the best and differentiate yourself in the community. At Root & Associates, we actually have a staff member assigned specifically to our client experience strategy. This person is responsible for monitoring client service, suggesting enhancements, and implementing changes.

Remember: if you don't ensure a rich client experience every time... who will?

CHAPTER 12

Building for the Next Generation

"Choose a job that you like, and you will never have to work a day in your life."

– Confucius

To this point, we have focused on building a different kind of business—one that supports the life you want to live, instead of dictating it. That business is a Next Generation Accounting Firm. By this point in the book, the elements that make up what a Next Generation Accounting firm is should now be clear. Take a moment to review the definition again:

> A business built on focused intention with unmitigated entrepreneurial spirit that enables you to have the life you want. It runs on a business model that supports an environment where you can be *present* in all aspects of your personal and professional lives to have the greatest impact on family, staff, clients, and community. A business that operates independent of you; creates a better working culture for your firm; offers security through recurring revenue; fosters creative thinking; evokes excitement with each new stage of evolution; inspires the next generation of professionals; and is built for transition to support your legacy.

Can you now start to feel what it means to build this type of business? Knowing all you know now, my hope is that you are experiencing some excitement around what your firm could be.

Getting back to the core focus of this chapter, building for the next generation, let's now move on to what this means.

Let's start by looking at the life you want to live. For me, and I think for most people, "the life you want to live" centers on one key area: security. Not only do I mean financial security for my family and my firm, but also the security of building a business that I can be proud of…proud to pass on to the next generation. A business that enables me to be an integral part of its overall success and still leaves me time to be present in all aspects of my life—family, staff, and clients.

It's also a business that presents me with the opportunity to stay involved at a strategic level and continue the work that I love, that requires my unique abilities, even when I decide it's time to transition. Security is possible at all levels if you build your business properly, which includes many elements—from a streamlined technology infrastructure and business model to developing a high functioning team. If you build your practice for the next generation, you, too, can experience the security that we all seek.

Building your firm for the next generation will not be easy. There are many changes, both structurally and personally, that you will need to make as you move down your continuum. I mentioned the issue of guilt early in the book, and I think it's important to mention it again as we come close to the book's end. Guilt will insert itself—sometimes viciously—into your transition. And while I believe this is natural with any major change, it's critical that you stave it off as best you can. The fact is that your mode of operation has probably remained steady for years. Working as a technician is likely the norm for you. Moving from a technician role into that of an entrepreneur is a major change, which often leads to guilt—guilt that you are abandoning a traditional part of your life; guilt that you are pulling yourself out of day-to-day tasks to work at a strategic level; and guilt, eventually, that you are working far less hours in your firm.

Guilt has been one of my biggest challenges, and one that I continue to struggle with today. As I work to stay focused on opportunities that have higher levels of impact on my business, there is always a pull—that guilt that I should be in the weeds getting technical work done. This is exceptionally true during tax season, when I tend to get pulled back into day-to-day work because I feel guilty delegating tasks that were traditionally my responsibility to focus on strategic work. Down deep, I knew that I was working. In fact, I knew that I was over-delivering on strategic work—the work needed to grow the firm and continuously increase revenues. This leads us now to the work you need to do to secure your biggest asset.

Securing the Future of Your Biggest Asset

Your firm, like mine, is likely one of your biggest assets, and certainly a shining example of your legacy.

Whether you're just getting started or you've been managing your firm for decades, you want to make sure that when the time is right, you can transition your professional heritage with ease. Whether that means stepping out of your business completely or staying involved at a strategic level, the time to prepare is now. Transitions are much easier and more enjoyable if you feel that all your security needs are being met.

The firm I operated 20 years ago was not the legacy I wanted to hand down to the next generation. The long hours and perpetual stress brought on by a heavy workload and unrealistic deadlines made me feel trapped—which did not meet my security needs or any semblance of work-life balance. I didn't want this for myself, and I knew I didn't want it for my children, should they choose to join me or run my firm some day. Because your firm is one of your biggest assets, you have to build it with transition in mind. And that means building a Next Generation Accounting Firm—a legacy you'll be proud to pass on and will meet your need for security.

Building your firm for the next generation—if it's done right—can also have a positive financial impact. As you probably know, the standard long-term rule of thumb is that a firm is worth up to approximately 1.2 times its annual revenue. You read that correctly, "up to." What you may not know is that a payroll business can be worth as much as 3 to 5 times its annual revenue. I have given this discrepancy a lot of thought. I believe a payroll business tends to hold more value because it's built upon a foundation of standardized systems and processes. When processes are uniform, they are easily repeatable and, therefore, are not dependent on a single person. Any employee trained on the system can operate it and process the work. On the flip side, accounting firms tend to be built around a unique individual—you. The asset then becomes the person and not the business, which buyers are less willing to pay for. Clearly, building a firm with transition in mind can be more financially rewarding.

Why is all this important? Because many firm owners are about to face the transition period of their careers. In fact, the AICPA reports that a large number of baby boomer practitioners are set to retire before 2024—roughly 75 percent. Those practitioners that build their firm for transition are not only securing the legacy of their biggest assets, they are also preparing for the opportunities that await. And our profession is on the verge of an unprecedented opportunity that will shape the future for years to come. I call this the Great American Accounting Opportunity™—so great, in fact, that it deserves a detailed description.

The Great American Accounting Opportunity

The statistics reported by the AICPA represent more than just a forecast of firms owners that may retire—they represent a major opportunity for three key stakeholders: universities and business colleges; young, newly minted professionals; and owners of small firms. Here is what each stakeholder stands to gain and the disconnects that have historically been obstacles:

> **Universities** have become conditioned to steer accounting graduates to large firms, largely because small firms don't have established inroads and communication channels with career placement offices. By connecting with small accounting firms, schools can link students with a greater depth and diversity of quality career opportunities.
>
> **Accounting students** are inundated with big firm propaganda from the beginning of their educational career. Young professionals who go to work for these large firms after earning their degrees often become restless after a couple of years and yearn for a work environment that promotes creativity and a

better work-life balance. But with a narrow worldview of our profession, they don't know where to look for their next opportunity. The majority has never seen or experienced small accounting firms, unless they have a direct connection, such as a family member (as I had). Introducing small accounting firms to young professionals opens up new opportunities for them to experience an entirely different side of the profession with a greater degree of self-determination—flexibility, work-life balance, competitive compensation, and even a pathway to ownership of their own businesses (entrepreneurship).

Small firms often operate in silos, detached from the larger worldview of our profession. They don't have sufficient time, resources, or perceived prowess to effectively recruit bright and talented young people from good schools. Not only does this create a vacuum of resources for firms in the present, it sets up an ominous threat to long-term sustainability, owner equity, and transition planning for small firms.

The Great American Accounting Opportunity will come to fruition when there is a platform to connect these stakeholders and bridge the communication and social gaps that keep us isolated from one another. If our industry is successful in doing this, we'll usher in a renaissance in our profession.

If you are part of the 75 percent forecasted to retire, the big question is: How are you going to address the next phase of your career? Retirement in full or in part? You really do have a choice. Why not capture more of the market, taking over for those who choose to simply close their doors at retirement? If you build your firm for the next generation, this is a realistic goal.

Now, let's take a look at the three potential paths in front of you:

Shut it down. This option dictates simply closing the doors. You've worked as long as you can; you have no desire to sell your firm or pass it on, so you shut it down. Sadly, many practitioners who haven't been able to keep up with change choose this option as a way out. This option assures that you will get the least out of what could have been a highly valued asset.

Sell your interest to another firm or partner. Whether you have a partial or 100 percent interest in your firm, buyers want to purchase assets that are proven to be a good investment. If you've built a firm that depends completely on you, chances are that once you leave, many clients may go elsewhere as well—not a good investment for buyers. If you plan to sell your interest at any point in the future, the best way to maximize the value of your asset is to create a firm for which interested buyers are willing to pay a premium—and that's a firm that does NOT require you to be at the center of everything.

Evolve your work life. This option is not often considered, but should be. Evolving your work life simply means setting up your business to be less dependent on you to ensure a smooth succession. Consider for a moment that you've made the effort to transform your practice into a Next Generation Accounting Firm. With a firm that operates efficiently and profitably, you now have an asset of greater worth. Not only is your firm worth more on a monetary level, but it also allows you to choose your level of succession—partial or full. I encourage you to know that, while it will be a lot of work, you can do it. Tomorrow is a new day, and you can decide to do things differently. Just like our personal lives, where we pass through phases from youth and family to empty nesters, your business moves through phases of change as well. I'm at the point in my career where I desire more freedom, and I have it because I made the effort to evolve my work life so that I can live the life I want—and still reap the benefits of a highly profitable business.

Regardless of your goals for the future, building a business that provides you the flexibility to live a happy and fulfilled life and maximize the value of your firm should be your goal.

For the next generation of professionals, The Great American Accounting Opportunity applies as well. With so many firm owners scheduled to retire, the market is wide open for new blood, energy, and vision. And while some of these up-and-comers may choose to open their own firms from the start, most will be looking for opportunities to grow within a small firm…with aspirations of making partner and taking over operations in the future. With that in mind, established firms that plan to take advantage of the coming opportunities should think about building an ideal team—the team that will support a business independent of any individual. Looking to the next generation of professionals is where you'll find individuals to build your well-oiled machine.

Now, let's talk a bit about the next generation of professionals. I think it's important to clear up a few misconceptions before we proceed.

Over the past few years, there has been much discussion among the accounting profession's thought leaders regarding young professionals. I hear again and again that today's young professionals are "significantly different." This consensus certainly isn't earth shattering. After all, what generation isn't different from its predecessors?

Unfortunately, part of this mindset among established practitioners is negative—postulating that the younger generation doesn't want to work as hard, or that young accounting professionals don't embrace the traditions of the profession.

I'm here to tell you, confidently, that I disagree with this synopsis completely. True, the next generation is different. But the key to most of our differences lies in technology. The 20-somethings have grown up with advanced technologies as an integral part of life. A high-tech, highly efficient world is what they know, so they expect to work in an environment that mirrors this. The next generation is made up of digital natives who are used to collaborating in real time and being connected 24/7. They don't want to sit behind a desk and churn out returns, but instead desire to work within a highly advanced infrastructure, complete with all the conveniences of their technology-driven personal lives. It's not that the younger set doesn't embrace the traditions of the profession; they do. They simply want to uphold professional traditions within a culture of exceptional efficiency and innovation. And as a Next Generation Accounting Firm, so should you.

This leads to the next big question: How do we attract the best-of-the-best from the next generation pool? If your plan is to continue operating the same as usual, then this task will be difficult. If you are on board to continue the journey to Next Generation Accounting Firm status, you'll be far better positioned to attract quality professionals to augment your biggest asset.

Today's technology offers a world of opportunity to build an advanced internal infrastructure that allows us to work any time, anywhere, and from any device—what our successors desire in their ideal work culture. The physical office is really no longer necessary, and geographical boundaries are a thing of the past. This is what will attract the younger set to your business and motivate them to stay for the long term.

To help you better understand the mindset of the new generation, I asked my daughter Meredith to explain her career goals and needs in a letter that I could share with you in this book. A 20-something with a Bachelor of Science and Master of Business Administration in accounting, and firmly entrenched in the accounting profession already, she is my lens into the young professional's way of thinking. As you consider the question, "What can I do to attract qualified young professionals to my businesses?" Get your answer by listening to what they have to say.

To offer a complete picture of what young professionals are looking for, I asked Meredith to supply responses in relation to several topics, including work culture, firm image, technology, and collaboration. She provided this in the following letter.

Dear Dad,

I wanted to write you a quick letter to let you know where I am in my career and update you on some of the decisions I've made.

Having worked for a Big 4 firm for a few years, I feel really good about the experience I've gained and realize the potential of a great career path. I've had the opportunity to travel the world and learn what it's like to be part of this profession. I do talk to my peers, and it seems like many of us are in the same boat. A lot of us are ready to move on—to use the experience we've acquired and put it to use in a more creative and flexible work environment. I remember you telling me that you went through the same thing back when you first started and were working for a big firm. The feeling within a larger firm is a lot like working on an assembly line, taking orders and fulfilling requests, one after the other. It's long hours that take away from my personal life, which stymies me from really being able to map out my destiny or to have consistency in my life. The bottom line is that I want a life, and that's why I feel like I've reached a point of transition.

There are many reasons why the small firm culture is so attractive to me. Getting my life back is the main criteria. And I know this is possible outside the world of the large accounting mindset. Here are a few things that I (and my peers) are really looking for as we search for new opportunities:

A business that supports a balanced life. Growing up, I always knew two things: I want to have a successful and fulfilling career where I'm challenged and I want to have a family. I want to be a part of a firm that will encourage me to improve and grow, but is flexible enough for me to take the time to raise a family. Work-life balance is something my generation expects. I want to work hard and one day run a great firm, but I also do not want to miss my child's basketball game or dance recital. Being a woman in this profession puts this topic even closer to my heart. In today's world, I know it's possible to have both.

A creative culture and powerful brand. As a creative professional, I want to work in a culture that fosters innovation and promotes creative engagement. This type of firm offers the opportunity to help shape the brand and a sense of ownership and pride in elevating business success. Throughout college and in my current position, I often heard the phrase "build your own brand," but this doesn't extend beyond me. I want the opportunity to build a professional brand; that's what gets me excited to work. Tapping into my creativity enables me to be more than a front-line worker in a firm; it gives me the opportunity to get into the mindset of an entrepreneur and help shape the business with purpose.

A highly advanced digital environment, primarily in the Cloud. I can't imagine working in a non-digital culture. My generation requires this level of connectivity, with the ability to work anywhere we want. My generation is about the iPhone and iPad, always connected. Firms that operate on a strong foundation of technology are able to support automated processes and consistency. This is how I want to work. This is the type of firm that I would choose to be part of—one that operates at the highest level of efficiency. My generation knows the power of being digital and how it impacts both day-to-day tasks and interactions with clients.

A highly collaborative environment. Throughout my years as a student at Indiana University, the majority of my assignments were team-based. In my current firm, I work in a team every day. That's because my generation is team-oriented. Collaboration drives creativity and a better work product in the end. Working together for a common goal often leads to an idea that surpasses the work one person could accomplish alone. A team environment uses the strengths of each individual and fosters engagement. I want to work in a business that is operated by a team, not solely dependent on one person. A collaborative work environment drives work-life balance and a staff that is on the same page. I can't imagine working in an environment of isolation; that simply wouldn't work for me, or most of the young professionals I know.

I truly believe that the time is right for the next generation of professionals to embrace their entrepreneurial spirit. Our first step is to work within a progressive, forward-thinking firm, where we can learn the ropes to one day run a successful business on our own. It's just a matter of finding the right firm...one that will enable me to create my own destiny...to have the life that I really want.

Talk soon,

Meredith

As you can see from Meredith's comments, we have a great opportunity to bring the next generation into our businesses—to embrace their passion and capitalize on their energy and dedication to the profession.

I realize that tradition is important, but the profession, like anything else, must evolve to survive. For years we've been a heads-down industry, focused on technical tasks and compliance. But the traditional mode of operation is not sustainable, and it will never deliver a highly profitable business, work-life balance, and the ability to choose your retirement path and enter succession with ease. To get to this point, it's a necessity to build a firm for the next generation, and this includes our technology-driven successors.

It's never too early to build a firm that is attractive to the next generation that also offers you the security you desire. Think of yourself as a mentor to these new and highly passionate professionals. As you evolve and change your role within the organization over the coming years, it will benefit you greatly to mentor those who may someday take your place and allow you to choose the succession path of your choice. Whether you want a firm that you can sell, or you are like me and want a firm that enables me to evolve with life's changes, it's never too early to get started down your evolutionary path.

CHAPTER 13

Change the Behavior...Change Your Game

Now that you've reached the last chapter, my hope is that you are thinking about your business differently—that you have adopted a true entrepreneurial mindset—because there has never been a better time in our profession to be an entrepreneur.

Only with an entrepreneurial outlook can you begin to think differently about your practice...to envision it as a separate entity from yourself...and start building a business that will support the life you desire and deserve.

Chances are that as you finish this book, you're still stuck in the weeds of your practice, plugging along from deep in the technician trenches. That's okay for now; after all, you are at the beginning of your journey. I've talked a great deal about this journey being on a continuum—your progressive path toward next generation status. That said, it's important to remember that this is not an all-or-none proposition. Any progress you make moves you closer to your vision. It's about progress, not perfection.

The most important work you can do to begin your transformation is to create your vision—to start with the end in mind. Your vision will serve as your compass as you make progress and move down the continuum. With a clear vision, you can begin to check items off of your list and move forward with confidence. Let's review each broad item once more:

Develop your business model. This will serve as the blueprint from which you and your team work to accomplish the goals you have set within your vision, including building the ideal client base and service delivery model.

Transition your focus to tasks that allow you to apply your unique abilities and have a greater impact on your firm's success. This will free you from time-draining technician work that yields no true value in growing your business.

Build your ideal staff. If you ever want to be free of daily technician work, you must develop a staff that can run your firm with or without you there. Training your staff on processes and systems takes time and effort. Build the right team and your freedom will come.

Create a powerful brand presence. This starts with your logo, and will boost your confidence immediately and put your best foot forward.

Implement your web and mobile strategy. This is essential to elevate your business as a powerful online force and provide the level of service today's clients demand.

Implement your marketing communications program. Ensure that you are communicating appropriately with clients and prospects and keep your sales funnel full.

Create a rich client experience. The client experience is at the heart of your brand, so take time to define your firm's client experience from the viewpoint of the client, not the firm. An exceptional client experience will work wonders in building a powerful brand and bringing in referrals.

Plan for successful execution. In all that you do during your journey, ample planning is required to execute successfully. Without planning, you run the risk of running an unintentional firm, which is, in large part, why you are where you are now—overwhelmed and ready for change. Be diligent about planning as you move forward. From my own materials and mailing.

Printed advertisements. Although you'll more often produce advertisements for specific publications as needed, it's handy to have a few on hand to take advantage of advertising opportunities that arise on short notice. Be sure that these "standby" ads are focused on general awareness of your brand so they can be deployed in a variety of different situations. Having these in electronic format is advisable, as publications may need to resize them for you.

We give you the tools, technologies and unparalleled support to take your business to the next generation.

Advanced technology, thought leadership, best-in-class service—a nationally recognized accounting firm to take your business through the next generation of change. Get started with Root today, and discover advanced solutions for back office administration, accounting, bookkeeping, tax management, payroll and more, all designed to benefit your work-life balance and your bottom line.

Learn more at **root.com**

Root & Associates 1516 South Walnut Street, Bloomington, 812.332.7200 (phone) **root.com**

One of my firm's print advertisements for publications in our service area.

Electronic presentation. You should have a professional slide deck available to tell your story to people at the boardroom table or gathered at an event. It's worth it to have a graphic designer help you develop the visual framework for your presentation to give it a professional, polished appearance. When you put together slide presentations, remember to keep them simple and sharp. Use the visuals on the screen to support what you say, rather than spelling it out in endless slides packed with text. Remember, a picture is worth a thousand words.

experience, I can say with absolute certainty that connecting with a like-minded peer group, where members are moving down the same continuum, is the best way to move forward with confidence.

Only Behavior Changes the Game – Do it With Intention

Everything you need to make your journey successful is within your reach.

It's now up to you to be intentional about your business—to take back the reins and chart your Next Generation Accounting Firm course. The time has come to give up your role as technician and start living and working as an entrepreneur. I realize that you've likely been working a certain way for many years and that change is difficult. Going against the traditions of the profession, perhaps everything you've known, can feel exceptionally uncomfortable. But the fact remains that if you don't change your current way of doing business, you will never achieve the life you want to live.

Albert Einstein said, "Insanity is doing the same thing over and over again and expecting different results." This is how I lived for years... steeped in insanity. It's your choice to stop the insanity today. The start of your journey begins with changing your mindset and changing your behavior. Only with a true shift in both can you change the game. It's time to be intentional.

If you haven't developed your vision...write it down. If you don't have a business model...develop one. If your clients aren't the right ones... go out and get them. If you are not happy with your brand...build a new one. If you don't have a systemized technology infrastructure in your firm...implement it. If you're not regularly planning...start today. Change the behavior...and you change the game.

I am confident that there has never been a better time to be an Intentional Accountant, building your intentional firm.

Made in the USA
San Bernardino, CA
10 June 2014